OUR LIVING TRADITION

OUR LIVING TRADITION

Fourth Series

Edited by

Robert L. McDougall

Published in association with

Carleton University by

University of Toronto Press

The quotations from the work of Saint-Denys-
Garneau are from his *Poésies complètes* (1949)
and his *Journal* (1954) and are reprinted here
by the kind permission of La Corporation des
Editions FIDES, Montreal, and the Librairie
Beauchemin Ltée, Montreal, respectively. The
poem, "Emily Carr," from *Friday's Child* (Copy-
right 1955 by Wilfred Watson) by Wilfred Watson,
is reprinted here by the kind permission of Faber
and Faber Ltd., London, and Farrar, Strauss, and
Cudahy Inc., New York.

CONTENTS

INTRODUCTION

The lectures which follow were delivered at Carleton University between January and March of 1961 as the fourth instalment of a continuing series entitled "Our Living Tradition." In my introduction to the second and third series (published together by the University of Toronto Press in 1959) I described how the series as a whole came into being and what it set out to do, and I really have nothing important to add to or take away from what I said then. The heart of the matter was and is the meaning in this context of the word "tradition," and the association with it of the word "living." But the accumulation of twenty-six lectures in the three volumes published to date should have removed the necessity for anxious explanation. It will be clear that these studies are not meant to constitute a hall of fame where portraits of greatness are hung in the most favourable light possible and in relation to some preconceived notion of a Canadian way of life. The better analogy, appropriate to the setting of a public lecture programme, is the analogy of speech. The lectures constitute a dialogue through which is effected an exchange of ideas between the present and the past in Canada. The voices which take the initiative in the conversation are scholarly voices, yet the tone is not quite that of the learned journals. As is the case in good conversation, which is flexible and idiosyncratic, each lecturer chooses his own ground and pursues with vigour the direct or it may be the oblique and in this sense partial view that for the moment commands his attention. In the end is achieved what was intended: the creative interaction of a wide range of present-day minds and sensibilities with the testimony which men and women of earlier times have written conspicuously into the record of the developing life of the nation. Tradition, then, does not in this context mean the embalming of national stereotypes. It means process: the process, carried out on a person-to-person basis, of meeting, illumination, and discovery. How else describe this shifting vital conjunction of present and past than as something that lives?

Having read what the seven lecturers of the present volume have to say, and perhaps their nineteen predecessors, the reader may of course fall to thinking about what they have to say collectively about the national image. In the midst of the current almost obsessive concern for the national image, I think it is a good thing that the material will be found to yield its returns reluctantly and will frequently give the lie to easy generalizations. The search for identity, in so far as it is a necessary national pursuit, is the better for being difficult. The papers, on the other hand, unquestionably invite synthesis at the level of national values, Canadian or *canadien*. The Institute, however, considers it no part of its role as sponsor that it should draw lessons from the contributions to the series. Hence my perhaps exasperating refusal to so much as attempt to string the lectures on a common thread. That is a job for other hands, or my own hands in another capacity.

The "Living Tradition" series lay fallow in 1960 to make possible the sponsorship at Carleton of an interdisciplinary seminar on the "Angry Thirties," and from this circumstance, which in the event proved most welcome as a change of pace and an opportunity for experiment, has emerged the decision to offer the series in future only in alternate years. Amongst reviewers of the volume of 1959 there were a few who expressed misgivings about the continuation of "Our Living Tradition"—the argument being that the vein of "greatness," though admirably explored thus far, was wearing thin and would soon run out. But since, as I have explained above, the conception of a hall of fame is quite foreign to the Institute's purpose, we shall, I hope, be forgiven if we disregard the implied advice.

Robert L. McDougall, Director
The Institute of Canadian Studies
Carleton University, Ottawa

June, 1961

CONTRIBUTORS

J. M. BECK is Professor of Politics at the Royal Military College of Canada in Kingston. He has written numerous articles on aspects of Canadian government and is the author of *The Government of Nova Scotia*, which was published by the University of Toronto Press in 1957. He is at present collecting material for a book on the later period of the life of Joseph Howe.

DESMOND PACEY is Dean of Graduate Studies and Head of the Department of English at the University of New Brunswick. A New Zealander who came to Canada in 1931, he holds degrees from the University of Toronto and from Cambridge, and was elected a Fellow of the Royal Society of Canada in 1955. Two books, *Creative Writing in Canada* and *Ten Canadian Poets*, and his frequent contributions to periodicals, identify him as a major voice in the criticism of Canadian literature.

STANLEY R. MEALING, who has been interested in Simcoe's career for nearly a decade, was born in British Columbia and brought up in Alberta. He studied history at the universities of Alberta, Oxford, and Harvard. He is Assistant Professor of History at Carleton University.

ROBERT ELIE, novelist, dramatist, and critic, is director of l'Ecole des Beaux-Arts de Montréal. Saint-Denys-Garneau was his friend and a witness to his first efforts as a writer. After Garneau's death he collaborated in the publication of the complete works of the poet.

M. S. DONNELLY has taught Political Science at the University of Toronto, at the University of Saskatchewan, and (for the past ten years) at the University of Manitoba. A frequent contributor to the learned journals in his field, he has been working for the past two years on a biography of John W. Dafoe.

ROY DANIELLS has recently returned from a year's study in Europe to resume the chairmanship of the Department of English at the University of British Columbia. His interests are Milton, Baroque, and Canadian and Commonwealth literature, and he is the author of a volume of poetry entitled *Deeper into the Forest*.

ANDRÉ LAURENDEAU from his earliest days has been associated with French-Canadian nationalism; Groulx, Minville, and Bourassa were his mentors. His connection with *Le Devoir*, of which he is now editor-in-chief, began in 1947. He has been a member of the Quebec legislature, writes plays for television and theatre, and is a contributor to *Ecrits du Canada français*.

OUR LIVING TRADITION

J. M. BECK ON

JOSEPH HOWE

To the Council of Twelve and the Halifax oligarchy Joseph Howe was a dangerous radical who delighted in unsettling existing institutions. To Principal G. M. Grant of Queen's University he was a natural Tory who could never shake off completely his inherent conservative tendencies. To Professor Chester Martin he was remarkably like an English Whig with strong Burkean overtones. But the plain fact is that Howe was an independent to whom no political label can be attached. Furthermore, he would have liked it this way, for he wanted above all to be known as the educator in public affairs of the Nova Scotians of his day.

To assist him in this endeavour Howe was plentifully endowed with the attributes which were so lacking in Edward Blake, the subject of the first lecture in the first series of "Our Living Tradition." In that lecture Professor Underhill introduced Blake as "a painfully reserved and shy individual with no capacity for playing the demagogue," who detested public performances in which he was required to seek the applause of the crowd, who lacked "the thick hide which the politician needs in order to survive," and who derived little exhilaration or inspiration from the exercise of power. In all these respects Blake and Howe were poles apart, and, perhaps needless to say, while Blake was a tragic failure when he sought public support for his ideas, Howe usually succeeded in converting the electorate to his line of thinking.

The Tribune of Nova Scotia is indeed the correct appellation for Howe, for it is altogether astonishing how much of his energy

3

was devoted to the persuading of masses of people from the public platform. For a dozen years after 1836 he extolled unceasingly the advantages of free political institutions; after 1850 he kept urging public support for the building of railways as public works; by 1857 he had commenced a crusade against a Catholic "conspiracy" which, to his mind, was threatening his province's free institutions. Something of a lull occurred in the six years after 1860, for although he served as premier until 1863, the politics of the day were deficient in the great themes upon which the Tribune of the People liked to expound eloquently to the freeholders of Nova Scotia, while in the following three years he acted as Imperial Fishery Commissioner and was therefore debarred from active participation in public affairs. But politicking was in his blood, and in 1866 he was again on the hustings, this time to urge that the impending union with Canada was not the proper destiny for Nova Scotians. Compelled to admit defeat after two years, he then sought to persuade his compatriots to accept Confederation and to work its institutions to serve their own interests.

Howe's preparation as an educator of public opinion was unorthodox, to say the least. Certainly formal education played little or no part in the process. To his father—old Loyalist John Howe—he owed his familiarity with the Bible, his fondness for reading, and, in his own words, his "knowledge of Old Colonial incidents and characteristics." While apprenticed in the printing trade between the ages of thirteen and twenty-three, he spent his nights reading Shakespeare and anything else which came to hand, often to the point of endangering his eyesight. Occasionally he lamented the lack of books, but always he consoled himself that "the world is before me—a library open to all—from which poverty of purse cannot exclude me—and in which the meanest and most paltry volume is sure to furnish something to amuse, if not to instruct and improve." Indeed, he came to the conclusion that circumstances taught him better than books; that to learn to reason and act with clearness and energy he had to put himself into situations which compelled him to do these things as often as possible. In particular, he welcomed association and collision with highly cultivated minds as a means of trying out what was in himself and making it more fit for use.

4

In 1827, at the age of twenty-three, he became joint proprietor of the *Acadian,* and his self-education proceeded apace. As he himself put it:

> I shall soon become a perfect Quidnunc. I already read papers by the dozen—write long leading articles upon subjects about which I know nothing and speculate most gravely upon political changes, affairs of state, and all the varying accidents by flood and field which come within the reach of my good quill. When tired of editorial restraint and its attendant cant and humbug I put on the revered wig and sober phiz of Fred Maple and ramble along in my own way—or perhaps mount Pegasus and gallop a distance of four or five verses which you may occasionally see signed with four stars.
>
> (Letter, May 19, 1827, George Johnson Papers)

After a year with the *Acadian* Howe again broadened his responsibilities by assuming the sole proprietorship of the *Novascotian* in 1828. Under his guidance its circulation rapidly increased. Actually, Howe was fortunate in that this was the heyday of what a former Provincial Archivist of Nova Scotia, Dr. D. C. Harvey, has called "the intellectual awakening of Nova Scotia" (*Dalhousie Review,* 1933). Dr. Harvey pictures Nova Scotians as rubbing the sleep out of their eyes after 1812, until by 1835 they were thoroughly awake, and concludes that, without minimizing the achievements of Howe, the latter must be regarded more as "the embodiment of the spirit of the age" than as "having sprung Minerva-like from the rocks of the North-West Arm." As a result of this awakening, the products of the printing press had a ready market.

In a sense Howe was equally fortunate that so many of his subscribers were delinquent in their payments; for it was in search of subscribers and subscription fees for the *Novascotian* that he made his celebrated rambles throughout Nova Scotia. Materially the results were often unrewarding; once, having been gone eight days and ridden more than two hundred miles on horseback, he had only seven pounds as a reward for his labours. Yet in other ways the results were of untold benefit; between 1829 and 1835 he visited every section of Nova Scotia and gained a knowledge of its physical attributes and an insight into its people which few Nova Scotians before or since have possessed. He forgot little of what he had learned on these trips; it all stood him in good stead later. As I have pointed out in another context (*Canadian Historical Review*, 1960), here already was revealed "the restless, inquiring spirit that was Howe." To the end of his days "he was actuated by an irresistible drive to see, to know, and to participate. Wherever he went he took with him an almost insatiable curiosity to observe every form of endeavour at close hand. Once having seen and learned, he was eager to offer his views to the responsible officials, even though the matter was no concern of his."

For the moment he regaled his readers with accounts of his rambles. But he also provided them with "Legislative Reviews" in which his sympathy for the popular cause became increasingly apparent. He had started out as a mild Tory, a defender of the existing system of government; the son of John Howe could hardly have been anything else. But by 1830 Jotham Blanchard and the Pictou scribblers of the *Colonial Patriot* had converted him from the error of his ways; he became a constitutional reformer.

It took another five years and a celebrated libel suit to project him into the virtual leadership of the Reform movement. By that time his editorial comments on the real governors of the province, the Council of Twelve, had earned him their violent antipathy. Towards one group of their satellites, the magistrates who carried on the government of the city of Halifax, he was particularly harsh; he denounced "the hardship, inequality, and oppression of the assessments, the disposition of the fire taxes, the miserable but costly corruption of the Bridewell and Poorhouse, the inefficiency of the police, the malpractices of the brick-building, the delay of justice in the commissioners' court, and the confusion of the accounts" (J. A. Chisholm, *Speeches and Public Letters of Joseph Howe*, I, 59). Not only that; he published the letter of a friend which accused the same magistrates of corruption itself. The sequel was Howe's defence of himself in the Supreme Court on a charge of criminal libel. He described the occasion afterwards with obvious relish:

The scene in the Court House beggars all description. It was crammed to overflowing, and as hot as a furnace. For six hours and a quarter I defended myself and scourged my prosecutors, in a style that of course I was too busy to judge of, but which startled and astonished

6

the multitude who devoured every word like manna, and what was better awed the Bench, scattered and confounded the prosecutors, and what was best of all convinced the Jury.

(Letter, March 17, 1835, George Johnson Papers)

He knew, when he had finished, that the prosecution could not succeed, for "one old fellow in the box cried like a child"; he knew also that he could talk convincingly to the people of Nova Scotia. The next year he won a seat in the Assembly and embarked on a career where he could use the art of persuasion to the full.

By this time the intellectual awakening had reached the stage where Nova Scotians were eager to overhaul all the institutions of government. And so in his first session Howe found a majority of Reformers who, like himself, wanted the spirit of the British system fully applied—that is, a system of responsibility to the people extending through all the departments of government.

The British laws [said Howe] are modified to suit the condition of the colonies and we see no reason why British institutions should not be ... adapted to our situation ... in England the people can breathe the breath of life into their government whenever they please; in this country, the government is like an ancient Egyptian mummy, wrapped up in narrow and antique prejudices—dead and inanimate, but yet likely to last for ever. We are desirous of a change, not such as shall divide us from our brethren across the water, but will ensure to us what they enjoy.   (Chisholm, I, 104)

Already Howe was coping with the problem which would recur constantly—the relations between Nova Scotia and the mother country. Back in 1827, in the prospectus of the *Acadian,* he had extolled the blessings which accrued to Nova Scotia as part of the Empire and announced his determination to strengthen the British connection. His method was to keep his readers informed of public movements in Britain which were worthy of imitation. Thus Nova Scotians might be moved by the same impulses and develop along the same lines as Britons; "a Briton on this side of the water [would] feel himself ... the equal in every respect to a Briton on the Banks of the Thames or any part of the British Isles." In a very real sense Howe conceived the struggle for responsible institutions as one designed to make Nova Scotians truly British.

7

He insisted, however, that Nova Scotia ought not to delay the adoption of a sound principle until the Imperial Parliament set the example; "without reference to what may be done in other countries ... [we should] ascertain where the shoe pinches *us*, and having done so, with a firm hand remove the evil." Likewise, all the English practices ought not to be transported to Nova Scotia willy-nilly. Unlike Robert Baldwin in Upper Canada, he first dismissed the idea of converting the Executive Council of Nova Scotia into an English ministry holding office only so long as it retained the confidence of the Assembly: " ... this Province," he said, "is scarcely prepared for the erection of such machinery; I doubt whether it would work well here." He therefore proposed nothing more than an elective Legislative Council, hoping that two elective Houses might impose an effective check upon the irresponsible executive.

Yet once the Durham Report was published Howe became an early convert. "You ask me for the remedy. Lord Durham has stated it distinctly; the Colonial Governors must be commanded to govern by the aid of those who possess the confidence of the people and are supported by a majority of the representative branch." To accomplish this objective, however, he was unwilling to depart from a moderate course. The rebellion in the Canadas had filled him with absolute horror and engendered in him a lasting suspicion of Canadians. The strongest act he would support was an address to the Crown requesting the removal of the Lieutenant-Governor, Sir Colin Campbell. That act brought the Governor-General, Charles Poulett Thomson (soon to be Lord Sydenham), to Halifax, where he started negotiations for the type of ministry which was his peculiar contribution to colonial politics, one in which, as Chester Martin has put it, "the governor was to govern, and the Executive Councillors were to be the governor's 'placemen' ... diverting men's minds from awkward abstractions."

How could Thomson persuade the leaders of the contending factions to sit together in the Council and thereby submerge party feeling? Upon some Reformers his blandishments had little effect; Herbert Huntington, for example, fully understood that any Reformers who went into the Executive Council could have little influence if its conservative members clung to their old viewpoints. But Howe was easily won over. Perhaps it was the lasting influence of his father which was responsible; to the end John Howe had thought this the best of all possible worlds and doubted the propriety of hammering the great folks too vigorously. But more likely it was Howe's deep-rooted sense of loyalty which was the determining factor. Thomson had discovered the weak chink in his armour: simply convince him that it was his duty to assist in reducing discord and in setting an example for the rebellious Canadians.

So Howe was made to acknowledge that, while the Governor-General's system differed a little in theory from his own, it was in essence the same and in some respects better. How he was led to believe that the coalition experiment could ever realize the ends he had in view is altogether inexplicable. Genuine ministerial solidarity was an illusion from the start. As Howe later told Lord Falkland, what was absent was "the assurance of good faith ... of common sentiments, and kindly feelings, propagated through the friends of each, in Society, in the Legislature and in the Press, until a great Party is formed ..." Obviously no such development could occur under the coalition; the miracle is that it lasted from September, 1840, to December, 1843, before it collapsed.

With its breakdown Howe set to work to hasten the sharper delineation of parties which the coalition had arrested. To those who argued that the colonies lacked the great questions of principles which might form the touchstones of party, he replied:

"little things are great to little men," and to little Provinces, and I could point to a dozen [past] questions of internal policy ... and to a dozen [future questions] ... that were or will be of just as much importance to the people of Nova Scotia, as were the questions upon which ministers have come in and gone out in almost every reign since 1688. It cannot be otherwise in the very nature of things.
(Chisholm, I, 361)

He contended, too, that the materials needed to build up a Reform Party were readily available. On one occasion he offered to take a dozen young men from the forges in Halifax "who with a sledge-hammer in one hand and a hot horseshoe in the other, shall deliver a better speech on responsible government than [their opponents] can make after a month's preparation." But he relied mostly upon the sturdy yeomanry who had won their farms from the wilderness; among such as these Howe set out to generate a healthy tone of public feeling. Interspersed with practical farming in the Musquodoboit Valley which he loved,

he went through the Province electioneering, and firing every Nova Scotian heart. He did the work of three men and as many horses. One summer he addressed 60 meetings in 90 days, many of the meetings being in the open air, and lasting the whole day, as able opponents had to be met and answered. He could feel the pulse of a crowd in five minutes, and adapt himself to its sympathies. He was equally at home with the fishermen of Sambro, the farmers and shipbuilders of Hants, the coloured folks of Preston, and the Germans of Lunenburg. He would ride 40 or 50 miles, address two or three meetings, talk to those who crowded round him after the meeting, and spend the night at a ball or rustic gathering as light of foot and heart as if he had been idling all day.

(G. M. Grant, *Joseph Howe*, 62-3)

By 1846 he had thoroughly identified himself with public feeling throughout Nova Scotia. Lorenzo Sabine, in his *Biographical Sketches of Loyalists of the American Revolution* (I, 133), points out: "It was 'Joe Howe', by day and by night. The Yankee pedler drove good bargains in 'Joe Howe' clocks. In the coal mine, in the plaster quarry, on board the fishing-pogy, the jigger, and the pinkey, it was still 'Joe Howe'. Ships and babies were named 'Joe Howe'.... The young men and maidens flirted and courted in 'Joe Howe' badges, and played and sang 'Joe Howe' glees. It was 'Joe Howe' everywhere."

What was the secret of the spell which he cast upon his native province? Recent studies by Professor Keith Thomas (*Dalhousie Review*, 1959) attribute much of it to his oratory. George Brown may have surpassed him in the grand style, John A. Macdonald may have been a more brilliant tactician, but in other aspects of oratory Howe surpassed all the British Americans of his day. According to Professor Thomas, "he was a master of factual detail and its skilful presentation; in his smooth and effective transitions he possessed the last touch in structural skill; his astounding adaptability allowed him to persuade even a greater range and variety of audiences than those won over by the others; and his powerful rhythm could reinforce and make still more effective all his other qualities of persuasion." Is it any wonder, then, that "in arousing attention no matter where he went, in enforcing his arguments, in stimulating the imagination of his hearers, and in exciting their feelings," he had no superiors?

Yet his oratory was persuasive only because he had a genuine, almost passionate, belief in the principles which he advocated. No utterance of his is more characteristic than "I believe all monopolies are bad." His early battles against the Halifax Banking Company and the magisterial system of the capital city, his part in the struggle for responsible government, his attitude towards free trade, his conception of the status of colonies, his quarrels with the Anglicans, the Presbyterians, the Baptists, and the Catholics, his whole scheme of railway building, and even his attitude towards Confederation may be made to form one coherent pattern: an attack on monopolies and privileged interests which were preventing a free people from enjoying its natural birthright.

His suspicion of vested interests and his belief that the people must ultimately be the governors were closely linked with his intense and passionate love for his native province and his equally profound attachment to the mother country. To those who asserted that Nova Scotia "should not complain of slight grievances because we have so many benefits," he was quick to reply:

here is the country of my birth; this little spot between Cape North and Cape Sable is dear to me as a Nova Scotian above every other place; and, while priding myself in the glories of the empire, I respect, as a native should do, the soil on which I tread.

(Chisholm, I, 208)

But responsible government need not loose the Imperial tie either:

fairly and legitimately worked in North America, it will perpetuate our connection with Great Britain . . . I respect colonial secretaries and members of Parliament, but I abhor that spirit of tuft-hunting toadyism, which leads some persons to seek for infallible wisdom under a coronet, and to undervalue everything in our own country. . . .

(Chisholm, I, 590-1)

Thus Howe condemned the compact system because it was "a

reflection upon the intelligence and ability of the colonists," and insisted on self-government because it was "the undoubted birthright of the descendants of the men who had won it at home and because to be denied it was to be cut off from the best traditions of the British race."

August 5, 1847, became the testing-day of all this activity, and a day of victory as well. While the Reformers' majority was only seven, Howe called it the best Assembly in history because there were no "loose fish," no members who were willing to sacrifice a constitutional measure for a road vote. It was they who threw out the Tories, thereby permitting the first responsible ministry in the British overseas empire to be instituted in Halifax in February, 1848. Nova Scotia, Howe boasted, had become a model for the other colonies to follow in the way of constitutional agitation. But perhaps he was more than a whit smug and sanctimonious; certainly the rebellions in the Canadas played no mean part in permitting constitutional changes to be effected in Nova Scotia "without a blow struck or a pane of glass broken."

Now Howe was in a position to keep a promise to his friend Charles Buller; he had undertaken to "make Nova Scotia a 'Normal School' for the rest of the colonies"; it would prove that representative institutions might be worked to ensure internal tranquillity and advancement without detriment to the paramount interests and authority of the Empire. What were the political attitudes with which he approached his new responsibilities? Certainly he was not an ultra-democrat, even though the former Lieutenant-Governor, Lord Falkland, had regarded his familiarity with all sorts of people as certain evidence of it. Falkland, according to Principal Grant,

had been a Lord of the Bedchamber and what not in England, and he looked upon colonists as a kind of semi-savages that he had come out intending to be very kind to. Social equality he had never dreamed of. Yet here was an Orson, very strong, but a perfect brute, who would perhaps walk up the street arm-in-arm with a truckman, shake hands with him, and next minute enter Government House, and calmly offer the same hand to a Lord of the Bedchamber, husband of a king's daughter, as if a Lord was not very different from a truckman, and was on a level with Orson himself.... It was a terrible time in Nova Scotia. (*Joseph Howe*, 59)

But not so terrible; certainly Howe had no desire to turn the existing institutions upside down. He opposed universal suffrage when it was introduced in the 1850's; he helped to secure its repeal in the 1860's. Land was so easily acquired in Nova Scotia, he contended, that any person worthy of a vote could easily secure a forty-shilling freehold. Under universal suffrage "the small minority who make a trade of the franchise, who can be bought up, who have their debts forgiven—these are the people who carry the election."

Again, in his concept of the function of leaders and legislatures Howe was definitely whiggish. Eight or nine men sitting on red cushions and doing nothing but pocketing their salaries ought not to call themselves a government. "Those who aspire to govern others should neither be afraid of the saddle by day nor the lamp by night. In advance of the general intelligence they should lead the way to improvement and prosperity." When Howe talked about governing according to the well-understood wishes of the people, he meant the well-understood wishes of the intelligent, not the wishes of the uninformed. As to Assemblymen, he never considered them mere delegates of the people; "if the Legislature desires and enacts a good measure," he said, "clamours will subside, and ultimately the Act will be hailed with thanks and praise from one end of the Province to the other."

Now, to the practical application of these principles. Howe later talked about his conducting the successful administrations of Governors Harvey and Le Marchant between 1848 and 1854, and his critics have labelled this as sheer egotism. Certainly the leader of the government was J. B. Uniacke, but actually the principal business of the country was conducted in the office of Provincial Secretary headed by Howe, and in the eyes of Nova Scotians generally it was his administration, not that of the colourless Uniacke.

In effecting the changes needed for the practical implementation of responsible government, Howe's course was moderate, to say the least. He and his colleagues demanded only seven major offices, the smallest possible number required to implement their concept of responsible government. Before the incumbents were finally removed, he had become appalled at the tender solicitude shown for protecting the faintest shadow of claim which wealthy

13

individuals had upon the revenues. "Why, sir," he said ruefully, "the strongest man in this House would hardly be able to carry on his back the piles of remonstrances on behalf of these people that one after the other, packet by packet, went across the water."

These major offices were required, of course, for the members of a responsible Executive Council. Howe insisted that subordinate officials, as well, be brought directly under the control of the Executive Council. By the time he was through he might well say: "Our Deities of the olden time ... were immovable on their pedestals; now we can bowl them out like ninepins." But, despite the clamours of his supporters, he adamantly and successfully opposed the adoption of the principle "to the victors belong the spoils."

In another matter, however, Howe displayed the blind spot which he had revealed earlier. During the coalition, he had held simultaneously the Speakership of the Assembly and membership in the Executive Council, and even fellow Reformers criticized him for not recognizing that the Speaker's single duty was to protect the Assembly, if need be, against the government itself; now so many of his relatives seemed to get into subordinate offices that the *Acadian Recorder* talked about a "Joseph Howe compact." Somehow Howe felt that he need not be as circumspect in these matters as others, that because of his boundless sacrifices and his well-intentioned motives, he should not be judged by the same standards as his colleagues or his opponents.

Only two years were required to transform the political institutions to meet the Reformers' requirements. By March, 1850, Howe was already dreaming new dreams; for him the railway era had dawned. Have done with the "croakers and cravens" who distrust the energies of the province, he told a Halifax audience. Now that the great political questions had been settled, the people should look to the development of the country's resources. Public men ought not to rest on past accomplishments, but should "be in advance of the social, political and industrial energies which they have undertaken to lead." Some things governments should not touch or attempt to control, "but the great highways ... should claim their especial consideration."

The outcome was that in November Howe was in London requesting aid of the Nova Scotian portion of a railroad which

14

was intended to run to Portland, Maine—the so-called European and North American Railway. Little did the Colonial Secretary, Lord Grey, know what was in store for him when that "upstart" Howe first addressed him on November 12. That communication was completely orthodox. But then the irrepressible Mr. Howe chose to have one of those "flashes" which were his wont. Why not make the railroad part of a vigorous colonial policy which would include representation in the British Parliament for two Executive Councillors from every colony enjoying responsible government? His diary entry of December 1, 1850 indicates that the idea amazed even Howe himself: "never heard it suggested at home or here. Never thought of it myself before."

For three days he worked furiously, and on December 4 his grandiose plan was ready for submission with the somewhat ingratiating comment that if Grey would only accept his suggestions he might become the greatest of all Colonial Secretaries. As it was, said Howe, a Colonial Secretary was in worse than Egyptian bondage. In every administration he was the scapegoat, always on the defensive, surrounded by complaining colonists and speculating companies. Give him assistance in Parliament from two Executive Councillors from each mature colony, and he would no longer be the victim of a swarm of small-fry critics and pressure-mongers. The colonials who proved their worth might later be employed in Downing Street or as governors. This simple expedient would afford British Americans the same scope for honourable ambition as their American neighbours.

Howe promised to incorporate an intercolonial railway into his plan in a second letter. But the Colonial Secretary was unenthusiastic. The colonials, he reminded Howe, would hardly want representation at Westminster if it meant increased taxation, as it surely would. A further reverse occurred on December 28— Howe's so-called Black Thursday—when Grey denied a guarantee for the railway. By some miracle Howe managed to have the refusal suppressed and to secure permission to feel the pulse of the British public on the matter.

As a result, in his Southampton speech of January 14, 1851, he was in the unprecedented position of a colonial trying to persuade the British public to support his demands upon the British government. It was perhaps his greatest effort. "To reproduce England on the other side of the Atlantic; to make the children, in institutions, feelings and civilization, as much like the parent as possible, has been the labour of my past life," he began. Now he wanted to draw the ties closer, to the mutual advantage of both. By promoting colonial development England would provide an outlet for her surplus population, reduce her expenditures on poor relief, ensure a source of military and naval stores, and afford strong and grateful allies in times of conflict. The colonies would prepare the wild lands for settlement if only Britain would provide ocean steamers for the poor and promote public works through imperial credit. The result would be a new attitude of mind throughout the Empire. "We shall feel that England is indeed our home, and you will feel that you have homes on both sides of the Atlantic." How could the British public promote his ideas? "The responsibility in this as in all important measures rests with the people. Let them stimulate the Executive, if that is required."

The appeal was apparently successful, for on March 10 Grey seemed to accept the principle of a guarantee for both the Halifax-to-Quebec and the European and North American railways. "This closes the past up nobly," wrote Howe. "The future is full of labour and perplexity." Greater perplexity than he could ever have imagined. For one thing, Grey had accepted little of his concept of empire. Colonial representation at Westminster he had already spurned; the settlement of convicts in British America he described as impracticable; the transportation of emigrants he considered best left to private enterprise. Finally, when Howe suggested the setting up of a National Association under the patronage of Prince Albert to ensure that emigrants would get cheap lands, he became thoroughly annoyed. Here was this pestilential fellow Howe exaggerating the amount of destitution and unemployment in the United Kingdom and making the British government look bad. He replied sharply that there was little unemployed labour in Britain, that the railroad contractors and the local governments could encourage emigration, and that under no conditions would he countenance the proposed Association.

Howe, the educator of public opinion, now had his work cut out for him; he had to persuade Nova Scotians, New Brunswickers, and Canadians to accept Grey's offer. In Nova Scotia he simply said:

16

Refuse, and you are recreants to every principle which lies at the base of your country's prosperity and advancement; refuse, and the Deity's handwriting upon land and sea is to you unintelligible language; refuse, and Nova Scotia, instead of occupying the foreground as she now does, should have been thrown back, at least behind the Rocky Mountains. (Chisholm, II, 170)

Elsewhere his argument was that the railway would promote "the general elevation ... of the Northern half of the Continent in perpetual connection with the Mother Country in preference to Annexation to the United States." Everywhere his oratorical magic was crowned with success.

And then in December the blow fell; Grey informed him that he had never intended to guarantee any portion of the European and North American Railway to Portland. Howe felt grievously humiliated; in his mind the Colonial Secretary had given way to powerful financial interests within his own party. Whatever the truth, Howe emerged from the situation in a much better light than Grey.

In the unsuccessful effort to save something from the wreckage, Howe played little part. Rather he turned his attention to building the Nova Scotia Railway. Yet he who could always persuade rank-and-file Nova Scotians found it difficult to convince a Legislature riddled with cleavages. Not until 1854, when every alternative had failed, was his proposal to build the province's railways as public works by open public contract accepted. But now Nova Scotia was on its own, and Howe had to get most of the funds from Messrs. Baring Bros. & Co. With some bitterness he wrote Lord Derby: "When our system of railways is complete we shall probably feel towards the Mother Country as Johnson felt towards the patron who left him to struggle through a work of great magnitude and value, the weight of which a little judicious aid would so materially have lightened."

Howe became Chief Commissioner of the bi-partisan Board chosen to supervise the construction of the railways, and as such must be given considerable credit for the entire absence from this work of the jobbery and corruption which were so characteristic of the era. It has sometimes been said that the only figures which he understood were figures of speech. Yet his progress reports were models of lucidity; above all, they were the reports of one who, not content to remain at an office desk, constantly travelled up and down the railway.

Although rebuffed once, Howe had not given up his plan of Empire. His opportunity came in February, 1854, during the debate in the Legislature on a proposal for the union of British America. In place of such a union, Howe pleaded that the intellectual resources of the colonies be combined with those of the mother country for the government and preservation of the Empire. Towards this end he suggested, first, the representation of colonials in Parliament, and, secondly, the appointment of colonials to share in the government of the Empire. In the United States, he pointed out, the poorest man in the poorest state might win the highest national honours. "The sons of the rebels are men full-grown; the sons of the loyalists are not. . . . How long is this state of pupilage to last? Not long. . . . I will live under no flag, with a brand of inferiority to the other British races stamped upon my brow."

Look at the Colonial Office! Not a person in it had any personal knowledge of colonial public or social life. Look at the Governors! Invariably they were old officers and broken-down members of Parliament in every way inferior to leading spirits in the colonies. Talk of a union of the provinces! "What we require is union with the empire; an investiture with the rights and dignity of British citizenship."

In March, 1855, Howe heard of vacancies in the under-secretary-ships at the Colonial Office and requested an appointment as evidence of "a new policy by which the highest Civil employments of the Crown were to be thrown open to the Queen's Colonial subjects." Howe's biographer, James Roy, calls this the beginning of "one of the most humiliating and self-abasing dunnings of Downing Street on record." Admittedly, some of Howe's importuning is irritatingly ingratiating. But fifteen letters over a period of six years do not constitute a serious pressure campaign. Since three ministries and six Colonial Secretaries held office during the same period, special efforts were clearly needed to keep one's claims under active consideration.

Legitimate ambition appears to have been the driving force behind these requests. Howe's contacts with British statesmen had

18

led him to conclude that he was in no way their inferior: yet a colonist's career appeared to stop when he became a provincial minister. "I contend," he said, "that, having reached that point, he is hedged in by barriers that he cannot overleap. . . . that he has got into a cul-de-sac. . . ." To him responsible government had conferred only the partial rights of British citizens upon colonials. As a natural extension, the Empire ought to be organized to confer these rights fully. "To serve this Empire," I have written elsewhere, "was the noblest mission that he could conceive, preferably at its centre in London, but, alternatively, even in so remote and primitive a region as British Oregon."

Meanwhile Howe had embarked on a mission which was to lead inexorably to a conflict with the Catholics of Nova Scotia. This was nothing new; previously he had quarrelled with the Anglicans, the Presbyterians, and the Baptists. It was not that Howe was anti-religious. George Johnson, who knew him intimately, stated that "his bump of reverence was large," and his diary abounds with thanks to God who had crowned his labours with success. Nevertheless, his failure to accept the tenets of any particular denomination caused many good people to suggest that he join a Church and "consecrate himself to the Lord." Upon one of these self-appointed guardians he once turned angrily: "All the great truths of Christianity my Father taught me when I was ten years of age and continued to enforce till I was 30. I do not think that even you can add anything to the simple eloquence with which they were illustrated in his life and conversation."

His father's strict Sandemanianism he could not accept; yet its tenets influenced him in more ways than one. A Sandemanian was required to consider his property as liable to the call of the poor, and certainly Howe's assistance to the needy often left him in impecunious circumstances. Again, Sandemanianism, for all its rigours, was simplicity itself in its forms and tenets; could not Howe's resistance of anything in the shape of sectarian pretension or domination have stemmed from this source?

Howe began his career by exposing the exclusive claims of the Church of England; he was in the forefront of those who in 1851 repealed that provision which since 1758 had made the Church of England an established church in Nova Scotia. Earlier he had turned his sights on the governors of Dalhousie for seeking to give

19

that university a sectarian character by appointing three Presbyterian clergymen as professors and rejecting the distinguished Baptist, Dr. Crawley. In 1843 he let go at the Baptists, who for months had been attacking him because he favoured the withdrawal of government grants from the denominational colleges. "I deny," he said, "the necessity of sectarian colleges. . . . When I look abroad on the works of Providence, I see no sectarianism in the forest or in the broad river that sparkles through the meadows; and shall we be driven to the conclusion that men cannot live together without being divided by that which ought to be a bond of Christian union?" (Chisholm, I, 421.)

Finally it was the turn of the Catholics. The mid-century had ushered in that more inflexible brand of Catholicism which was inspired by ultramontanism. Nova Scotia had its first taste of it when, on March 17, 1854, a group of Irish priests started publishing the *Halifax Catholic*. From the outset it belligerently asserted that it would not stand idly by while the Irish Catholics of Halifax continued to be treated as second-class citizens. It heaped ridicule upon "that impalpable negation, that vague, ridiculous, inconsistent and unmeaning caricature, called Protestantism" and "those crawling creatures, those cramped intellects, those poor benighted Diggers, the Blind Baptists" (August 12, 1854). Politically it was violently anti-British, the woes of Ireland being a dominant theme, and in the Crimean War it was utterly unsympathetic to the British cause; England, it said, had "hatched plots, and encouraged treason, and subsidized rebellion in the bosom of almost every European state" (June 3, 1854).

These views must have been anathema to Howe, but he noted them without comment. Yet a complex chain of events had been set in motion which drew him almost irresistibly into conflict with the entire Catholic population. The match that set off the powder keg was Howe's futile but hazardous recruiting campaign in the United States from March to May of 1855. Though technically Howe may not have broken the American Neutrality Act of 1818, certainly he violated its spirit; yet to provide reinforcements for Britain's Crimean armies he was willing to go to almost any lengths, even to consorting with the lowest species of humanity, playing hide-and-seek with the police, and endangering his own good name.

Even the few recruits who arrived in Nova Scotia did not all reach the Crimea, for the Irish Catholics of Halifax persuaded the large number of their compatriots among them to go back on their bargain; some ended up as navvies on the Nova Scotia Railway. Furthermore, the Charitable Irish Society of Halifax, by giving publicity in the United States to Howe's mission, endangered its success. In this way there was built up a legacy of ill-will which was to erupt months later.

On May 26, 1856, a group of Irish navvies on the Nova Scotia Railway inflicted a merciless beating on some Presbyterian labourers from eastern Nova Scotia at Gourley's Shanty. Just ten days later—at a meeting to prepare an address to the British ambassador in Washington, who had been dismissed for his part in the recruiting campaign and who would shortly pass through Halifax on his return home—the Irish element raised violent objections. Both at this meeting and in the *Morning Chronicle* (June 10, 1856), Howe forcefully condemned the rioters and the extreme Irish faction in Halifax.

Of the Irish nation, or of the Irishmen in Nova Scotia, no man ever heard me breathe an ungenerous sentiment. But I am not blind to the national characteristics and foibles ... no people ... have suffered more from gross misleading ... there is scarcely a City on this continent where men with some fluency, and little judgment, have not embroiled the emigrant with the resident population.

So far Howe's quarrel had been with a racial, not a religious faction, and the Roman Catholic Bishop of Arichat assured him that the *Halifax Catholic* was far from being the exponent of politico-catholic views in his diocese.

The explosion burst in late December when a jury trying those accused of the riots divided along religious lines. A correspondent in the *Halifax Catholic* gleefully proclaimed that Howe's denunciation of the rioters had been responsible for the split jury. An accompanying editorial finally let the cat out of the bag; the riot had occurred because some Protestants had taunted the Catholic navvies for believing in the Real Presence of Christ in the Sacrament of the Eucharist; Protestants should realize how sensitive the Irish were to slurs on their religion or the character of their priests and exercise more caution in the future.

At this Howe saw red. Here was a group of people long associated with him politically, whose struggle for political, social, and religious equality he had supported for almost a quarter of a century. Now they too were developing pretensions of their own. Through the *Halifax Catholic* they had "week after week—scoffed at and reviled everything that British subjects value—everything that Protestant Novascotians hold dear. . . . They had written and acted as though Nova Scotians, who happen to be Protestants, had neither feelings, moral power, or political influence." Why should every Protestant in a free country not have the right to laugh at the doctrine of the Real Presence if he liked, just as every Catholic might ridicule the simple ceremonies which a Protestant deemed sufficient?

The right to discuss all questions or doctrines involving our worldly interests or our eternal salvation . . . and to laugh at what we believe to be absurd, is the common right of every Novascotian; and all the "mercurial" people that can be mustered will not trample it out of . . . our homesteads. (Letter by Howe in *Morning Chronicle*, Dec. 27, 1856)

The issue had now been joined on religious as well as racial grounds. Throughout January of 1857 the contest waxed hotter and hotter, and by the time the Legislature met in February Howe had lost the sympathy, not only of the Irish, but of the Acadian and Scottish Catholics as well; the result was that the seven Catholic Assemblymen and two Protestants representing Catholic counties deserted the Liberals and brought the Conservatives to power.

To Howe the moral seemed clear. Government deriving its energy from the people had come under "a dark and mysterious power, felt though unseen, and fatal to true freedom." In a letter to the people of Nova Scotia dated March 2, 1857, he proposed the formation of a Protestant organization to ensure the preservation of religious and civil freedom. His opponents derided the resultant Protestant Association as Howe's Know-Nothing organization; he himself, realizing that its formation was impolitic and injudicious, soon lost interest and the Association barely got off the ground. Shortly afterwards his opponents also moderated their extremism. Yet the issue still dominated the election which the Liberals won in 1859.

As for Howe, he never repented his part in the prolonged embroilment, even though his admirer, Dr. D. C. Harvey, has described it as "alien to his own character and instincts." But surely it is also possible to take the view that, however impolitic his conduct, it was certainly predictable and entirely in keeping with his character. These incidents touched two chords in Howe to which he responded instinctively—his loyalty to the Crown and his elemental sense of fair play. The response could not have been otherwise.

When Howe finally became premier of Nova Scotia in 1860, he can have felt no real elation; for all practical purposes he had served in that capacity years before. The next three years Professor Roy regards as a period of frustration. Certainly Howe must have questioned the wastage of the bitter partisan struggles and wondered if he had been right in contending that a small colony could develop the issues which would justify disciplined political parties based on principle. Nevertheless, he entered into his duties with his usual zest and displayed undoubted abilities as a tactician. In an evenly divided House in which Tupper moved heaven and earth to defeat him, he somehow managed to maintain the upper hand.

As an Imperial Fishery Commissioner from 1863 to 1866 Howe enjoyed many moments of leisure, and as usual he could not resist delving into public affairs. Once, when the American historian, George Bancroft, criticized Lord Palmerston and the British government, his reply was in such blistering terms that it was impolitic to publish it. But he devoted his major efforts to preventing the United States from abrogating the Reciprocity Treaty of 1854. In July, 1865, he achieved one of the major oratorical triumphs of his career when he persuaded the American and Canadian businessmen gathered in the Detroit Convention to resolve unanimously that the Treaty ought to be renewed. He may have convinced them by his eloquence on the relations which should subsist between Britain, the United States, and Canada:

Why should not these three great branches of the family flourish, under different systems of government, it may be, but forming one grand whole, proud of a common origin and of their advanced civilization? We are taught to reverence the mystery of the Trinity, and our salvation depends on our belief. The clover lifts its trefoil leaves to the evening dew, yet they draw their nourishment from a single stem. Thus distinct, and yet united let us live and flourish. Why should we not? (Chisholm, II, 439)

Meanwhile Confederation had come to dominate the political stage.

Some myths respecting Howe and Confederation ought first to be dispelled. One is that he did not attend the Charlottetown Conference because he could not bear playing second-fiddle to Tupper. In fact, Howe was under strong pressure from the Foreign Office to complete the work of his Commission with the greatest dispatch. Another myth, popularized by Principal Grant, attributes his stand on Confederation to his egotism: he could not tolerate the adoption of a scheme which he had not devised. Actually, on no issue did he feel more deeply; on no issue did he lavish more of his energies.

Any idea that his decision on Confederation was an impulsive one is also far off the mark. It is true that an interjection of his at a public meeting in Halifax on December 23, 1864, afforded the first clue to his thinking; it is true that he published letters anonymously on "The Botheration Scheme" in the *Morning Chronicle* between January and March, 1865; it is true that he revealed his opposition privately to the British government in the summer of 1865. But it is also true that none of these acts publicly committed him. Not until March, 1866, did he finally show his hand openly and participate actively in the anti-Confederation movement. For that decision he was to incur unimagined hardships.

When he became Fishery Commissioner in 1863, he had been in poor shape financially. His generous style of entertaining friends and associates, and his open-handed assistance to the poor—not mismanagement—were largely responsible. As he himself told the Nova Scotia Assembly in February, 1863, "I have earned a good deal of money by my private business, and in the public service, in my lifetime. Where is it? Back, as everybody knows, in the hands of my countrymen, from whom it was received." Three years of Imperial appointment improved his financial position considerably, and early in 1866, as it was drawing to a close, he

24

received a handsome offer to edit the New York *Albion*. He wrote
to Mrs. Howe on March 12, 1866: "It makes me feel more independent . . . than I have done for many a day." Yet at the same
time he was sorely troubled:

I am much inclined to accept [the *Albion* offer]—half inclined to
throw up everything, come home, and fight the battles of my own
country in the dark hours . . . closing round her. That would be the
right thing to do but we have had so much thankless care and labour
that I, for the first time in my life, hesitate between duty and interest.
Poor old Nova Scotia, God help her, beset with marauders outside
[i.e., Fenians] and enemies within, she has a hard time of it, and my
mouth closed and my pen silent.

Within days Howe was back in Halifax fighting Nova Scotia's
battles.

Finally, the oft-repeated remark that Howe had been a confirmed Unionist who deserted his beliefs is simply not true. Many
a time since the 1850's he had stated that colonial union should
not be considered until an intercolonial railway was built and
more contacts were established between the colonies. Now and
then, on convivial occasions, he had talked expansively on some
future union, but almost always he had indicated scant interest
in concrete proposals to that end. Howe might more fairly be
criticized because he refused to recognize the unhealthy state of
political conditions in all the colonies. His opponents argued that
by broadening the issues to be discussed and by making it worth
while for the best men to participate in politics, Parliament under
the Union would be a far healthier institution than the old
Legislatures. This argument Howe declined to admit.

Yet his stand should have been predictable because it was in
keeping with two of the dominant influences of his life. It is
true that his active mind eventually built up a massive list of
additional arguments; here, as on other occasions, his fertile imagination may have overextended itself. But basically he adopted
the position he did, first, because he wanted his compatriots to
have the right to say yes or no. The idea that the people are
ultimately the governors he put first among his political tenets;
certainly the people ought to be permitted to pronounce upon a

25

radical constitutional change which would affect them for all time to come. To take the side of coercion in this issue would have reversed all the principles for which he had fought. If Nova Scotians were tricked and bullied out of what they valued, they would never be content. Assuredly they ought not to be compelled to unite with a people like the Canadians, whose past record left doubts as to whether they possessed the spirit of tolerance needed to make British institutions work properly.

Equally important, the Union would take the minds of Englishmen and British Americans off what he considered the vital question of the time, the organization of the Empire. Since the early sixties he had been highly critical of the Manchester School of politicians, who talked of separation, and of other British politicans who criticized the colonies for not looking after their own defence. After he had laboured so long to prove that British institutions as well as a British population might be transferred to the colonies without loss of self-government, he was sorrowful at seeing the whole system "rudely shaken by speculative politicians, or perilled by such taunts and dissensions as have been of late too rife in England."

Now the Quebec scheme had come to endanger his concept of empire. While the provinces remained separated, all their ultra-provincial patriotism would go to the Motherland, but if fused into a new nation the old ties would be severed and republicanism would be the natural outcome.

London is large enough for me [said Howe] ... London, the commercial centre of the world, the nursing mother of universal enterprises, the home of the arts, the city of Empire, the fountain head of civilization.... London ... where personal liberty is secured by the decisions of free courts and where legislative chambers, the most elevated in tone, control the national counsels and guard the interests of the Empire.

(Memorandum by F. Blake Crofton, George Johnson Papers)

When, in 1866, Howe produced another paper on "The Organization of the Empire" for Lord Russell, he regarded it as a labour of love, "the result of ten years of reflection on the grandest subject to which an Englishman can turn his thoughts." On his own admission, his plans seemed visionary and impracticable, but only because nobody would grapple with the problem. His own position was unequivocal: "we should all go for the Empire, one and indivisible, as opposed to this policy of dismemberment."

Yet after immense efforts Howe had to admit defeat; the opposition was simply too formidable.

I have given two years to the battle for a repeal of the British American Act, at what personal sacrifice, perhaps, only I and my own family know. It has rarely fallen to the lot of any man to confront so formidable a combination. Arrayed against us were the Queen's name, the House of Lords and Commons, the Governor-General, three Lieutenant-Governors, thirty-five delegates, including many of the ablest men in British America, the Canadian press, and, until recently, nearly the entire press of England.

(Chisholm, II, 544)

Thus in mid-summer, 1868, Howe faced his most difficult decision. Some anti-Confederates wanted to accept Confederation as irrevocable; others were content to maintain and worsen their bad relations with Ottawa; a few talked wildly of annexation. Howe asked for direction from an anti-Confederate Convention, but received none.

He was on his own. But, as always, one basic consideration governed him: to keep Nova Scotia on a thoroughly loyal course. It was evident that if he made peace with Ottawa only part of the anti-Confederates would follow him; the remainder would regard him as a traitor. Nevertheless, after months of deliberation, he entered into negotiations with Ottawa for "better terms"; eventually he accepted Macdonald's pleadings to enter the federal cabinet as the best vantage point from which to pacify Nova Scotia. Many of his former friends were highly indignant. In the ensuing by-election in Hants they sent relays of speakers to contend with him in every polling district. Such rigorous electioneering in the dead of winter was too much for even his splendid physique. While he won the election, it left him a physical wreck.

As President of the Council and Secretary of State for the Provinces, Howe sought to make appointments in Nova Scotia which were calculated to promote the integration of the province into the Dominion. His old zest for travel remained. But a late autumn visit to the Red River to prepare for the admission of Manitoba as a province overtaxed his remaining strength. It left him without the physical stamina to perform his duties effectively.

Throughout these years his disillusionment with British legislators and politicians grew apace. He never forgave the British Parliament—to him the exemplar of all legislative bodies—for its indifference to the Act of Confederation: "I believed . . . that the House of Lords would do justice though the heavens should fall; that a man with a manly, honest face could go to the . . . Commons and obtain fair play." After that, he saw additional evidence of the dismemberment of the Empire, culminating in the sacrificing of Canada's interests by the Treaty of Washington. "Bit by bit England gives North America away," he lamented. Finally he stated openly that Canadians and Britons should soon have "a clear and distinct understanding as to the hopes and obligations of the future." This was not the prattling of an ailing and weary old man; it reflected the natural disappointment of one whose high concept of empire was being spurned, but also the confidence that British America, if forced to fend for itself, could make its own way. It is ironical that when Howe finally received a governorship it was the gift, not of the Colonial Office, but of the Dominion government. He had been installed in Government House in Halifax only twenty-two days when the end came on June 1, 1873.

This account of Howe may have treated him too sympathetically. It has, nevertheless, permitted him to demonstrate some of his own foibles: he could be ingratiating when it suited his own purposes; he was egotistical at times, although normally not obnoxiously so; he occasionally permitted himself a line of conduct which he would not tolerate in others. There were other deficiencies as well. For a time he would suffer abuse without comment, but when he finally took cognizance of it, he might show an utter lack of moderation. Self-educated in a hard school, he sometimes lacked refinement. Even in the Assembly his allusions were at times off-colour; with less sophisticated audiences he might stoop to outright vulgarity.

But, after all, these are minor blemishes. In Howe's career there is a basic consistency, an adherence to principles, which is uncommon. Criticize him if you will for his stand on the Catholic and Confederation issues, but nonetheless they reveal the true Howe. It is astonishing, too, that for a man who produced more ideas than any British American of his age he largely escaped the reputation of being an idle dreamer. Fortunately for him, the imaginativeness which came from his father was usually counterbalanced by the practicality which he inherited from his mother.

In what way is Howe significant in the "living tradition"? Actually, each element in him emphasized something which is now accepted. With the passing of an earlier optimism, realistic democrats today express views on leadership and the functions of parliament which closely approximate Howe's whiggish outlook. The view that the people must ultimately be the governors—a radical one in the 1830's and 1840's—is commonplace in modern liberal democracy. More particularly, the right of the electorate to give a prior approval to radical constitutional changes, upon which Howe insisted so strongly between 1866 and 1868, has become an established convention of the British constitution. At the other extreme, the conservative in Howe led him to proclaim his reverence for the past in language which will not be forgotten:

A wise nation preserves its records, gathers up its muniments, decorates the tombs of its illustrious dead, repairs its great public structures, and fosters national pride and love of country, by perpetual reference to the sacrifices and glories of the past.

(Chisholm, II, 619-20)

Howe is even more significant for his views on the external relations of the British American colonies. His statement of the ideal relationship which should subsist between Britain, Canada, and the United States has never been bettered. But above all, he must be considered one of the founders of the modern Commonwealth, even though his proposals for a centralized organization have been proved unacceptable. To some Howe may be primarily a Nova Scotian nationalist. But when he wrote in 1866: "I am a dear lover of old England and to save her would blow Nova Scotia into the air or scuttle her like an old ship," he was not suffering from self-delusion; his utterances over thirty years bear

29

a similar purport. He was in fact both a local and imperial patriot, who saw no difficulty in reconciling the two facets of his thinking. As he conceived it, Britain constituted a reservoir of values from which the colonies might borrow to advantage; with the development of the latter he expected the exchange to be a two-way one. That expectation has been fully realized. Again, the equality of citizens within the Empire which he advocated is considered by many to be the essential feature of the modern Commonwealth. The Commonwealth has, in fact, become what he hoped it would become: "a partnership, which may last for centuries, and need not terminate at all, so long as it is mutually advantageous."

DESMOND PACEY ON

SIR CHARLES
G. D. ROBERTS

A scant eighteen years ago, there appeared in the Ottawa *Journal,* from the hand of the late P. D. Ross, a review of Elsie Pomeroy's biography of Sir Charles G. D. Roberts, which read in part as follows:

Sir Charles George Douglas Roberts is a very great Canadian. If anyone should care to say that he is the greatest living Canadian, there is good argument for it.... Since his earliest maturity, more than sixty years ago, he has been pouring forth a flood of distinctive Canadian literature—poems, novels, nature stories, historical and general writing. The total production has come to more than forty volumes. Who can measure what effect this has had for good on Canadian life and thought?

(July 10, 1943)

In the same year, 1943, the late Professor Pelham Edgar wrote in the *University of Toronto Quarterly,* that "the poetry of Roberts ... is destined to endure all the fluctuations of taste and time. Here is no question of the ephemeral, but of the inevitable, once said and said forever." A series of such tributes could easily be listed, going all the way back to the eighteen-eighties when Roberts, still in his early twenties, was already recognized as the leading man of letters in the young Dominion. When Roberts was knighted for his services to Canadian literature in June, 1935, congratulatory letters poured in to him from all corners of the country: from fellow writers such as Morley Callaghan, Mazo de la Roche, E. J. Pratt, and Duncan Campbell Scott, from political

31

leaders such as Sir Robert Borden and William Lyon Mackenzie King, and from a host of ordinary men and women who saw in Roberts the very living embodiment of Canadian literature. To give just one more example, when in 1939 the young left-wing poet Dorothy Livesay wanted to rally Canadian writers to write honestly and directly about the life of contemporary Canada, she chose to address "An Open Letter to Sir Charles G. D. Roberts," then an old man in his eightieth year, stating "I address myself to you because you are a pioneer Canadian and a pioneer poet among us; because you have the tradition and the culture of our country at heart; and finally because your voice has not sunk to a whisper, but has come out boldly with the changing times. . . . Because you have given so much, we can still look to you to give more." (*Canadian Bookman,* April-May, 1939.)

Today, less than twenty years after Roberts' death, it seems that his reputation, which for sixty years seemed unassailable, is in danger of destruction. He still keeps a place in A. J. M. Smith's recently published *Oxford Book of Canadian Verse,* but he has only eight pages allotted to him as against ten for Isabella Valancy Crawford, twelve for Duncan Campbell Scott, twenty-three for E. J. Pratt, and eleven for Earle Birney. And even this modest allotment has been challenged by reviewers of Smith's anthology. Millar MacLure, in a recent review in the *Tamarack Review* (Autumn, 1960), has written contemptuously that whereas "Lampman is a good old cheese, Roberts and Carman belong on captions in the New Brunswick Museum." George Woodcock, in the *Canadian Forum* (November, 1960), recently complained that "it is laborious, except perhaps in nostalgia for the Edwardian afternoon, to read through as much of the Confederation poets as most anthologists, Dr. Smith among them, give us. Technical proficiency may begin with these writers, but the first really original presence among English Canadian poets is still E. J. Pratt."

A similar situation exists with respect to Roberts' prose. None of his novels has been recently reprinted, and his *History of Canada* does not even linger, as it well might, in the form of selections in school readers. Only his short stories have some surviving vogue: a selection of them, under the title of *The Last Barrier and Other Stories,* edited by Professor Alec Lucas, recently appeared in McClelland and Stewart's New Canadian Library, and an example of them is to be found in all of the recent anthologies of Canadian prose. One such anthology, Robert Weaver's *Canadian Short Stories* in Oxford's World's Classics series, is very recent, and it is significant of the probable trend that in one early review of that book the Roberts story is dismissed as being unworthy of inclusion. If Roberts' poetry does not survive, I think it very unlikely that his prose will.

Are we, then, to conclude that Roberts' place in our living tradition is now a dubious one at best? Was his work indeed ephemeral, over-praised, and essentially hollow? To answer this question will be the purpose of the remaining part of this lecture. But to answer it properly, and certainly to answer it in the terms of the title of this series, means setting Roberts in perspective, examining the traditions out of which he grew and the extent to which, if at all, these traditions may still be said to be "living."

I say traditions rather than tradition, for Roberts was in fact the product not of a single tradition but of several. There was first of all a family tradition. Whenever Roberts had occasion to mention the influences which affected him, he always gave first place to his father, Canon George Goodridge Roberts. In some brief manuscript autobiographical notes preserved in the Hathaway Collection in the library of the University of New Brunswick, Roberts has written: "What started? Brought up on father's knee —good poetry read to me—Tennyson, Longfellow, Byron—read for the music as often far over our head. About 8 or 9 made up mind was going to be poet. At 9 read Paradise Lost—it was a great Fairy story to me." His first book of poems, *Orion* (1880), was dedicated to his father, and he drew a very sympathetic portrait of him in his novel *The Heart That Knows* (1906).

Canon Roberts' interest in literature and scholarship is not surprising, for there was a family tradition of learning. The canon himself was a graduate of the University of New Brunswick, and served for many years as a degree examiner in Classics and French at that university. His father, in turn, the poet's grandfather, was a graduate of Oxford who was headmaster of the Fredericton Collegiate School for nearly half a century and acting Professor of Classics at the university during 1872-3. The poet's great-grandfather was also an Oxford graduate, and a scholar who compiled a Latin grammar and did a great deal of historical writing. When we add to all this the facts that the allied families of Goodridges and Gostwicks included many scholars and writers, and that Roberts' mother, Emma Bliss, traced her ancestry back to a prominent New England family which had intermarried with the Emersons, we can see that young Charles Roberts was predisposed by heredity and family environment to some kind of scholarly or literary career.

Even the most sanguine, however, might not have expected quite such a literary flowering as actually occurred in Charles' generation and in the generation that followed it. In addition to the work of Charles himself, there was in his own generation the poetry of his sister, Elizabeth Roberts Macdonald, the novels, short stories, and verse of his brother Theodore, and the extensive magazine writing of his brother William Carman Roberts. The productivity has continued into the present generation. The son of Elizabeth Roberts Macdonald, Goodridge Macdonald, is a practising Canadian poet of minor but real distinction; the eldest son of Charles, Lloyd, is a well-known poet and broadcaster; Theodore's daughter Dorothy is a good poet and the author of some fine short stories, and his son Goodridge is one of the best Canadian painters. Certainly there is no question but that in this respect Sir Charles Roberts is very much part of a *living* tradition. That it is a real, meaningful tradition, and not a mere accident of birth, can be seen by looking at the paintings of Goodridge. In their combination of tenderness and strength, in their loving particularity of detail, in their strong sense of design, in their subtle colouring, and in their combination of visual accuracy and spiritual insight, they have much in common with the best of his uncle's poems.

The second tradition with which I should like to deal is the provincial and civic tradition. I link the two, because it was largely the city of Fredericton, the capital of New Brunswick, that influenced Roberts, but not exclusively so. He was born near Fredericton, spent his early boyhood at Westcock near Sackville, and returned to Fredericton at the age of fourteen. After his education had been obtained at the Fredericton Collegiate School and the University of New Brunswick, he taught for a year at Chatham on the Miramichi, returned to Fredericton as principal of the York Street School, and, apart from a brief three-month interval in Toronto as editor of *The Week,* remained there until he became a professor at King's College, Windsor, in 1885. There was another brief interval of life in Fredericton in 1895 and 1896, so that altogether Roberts spent some twelve of his most formative years in the little capital city.

Now Fredericton, though a very small city of some seven thousand persons in Roberts' day, had much to offer to a young poet. For one thing, it had a literary tradition which went back virtually to its foundation. The first Provincial Secretary of New Brunswick was the lively Tory satirist Jonathan Odell, who from Fredericton sent out poems which found their way into the leading periodicals of England such as *The Gentleman's Magazine.* A little later, in the early decades of the nineteenth century, Julia Catherine Beckwith wrote in Fredericton the first novel to be published by a native English-Canadian: *The Nun of Canada* (1824). In the eighteen-sixties, Fredericton was the home for several years of Juliana Horatia Ewing, one of the most famous Victorian authors of children's books such as *The Peace Egg, Lob-lie-by-the-fire,* and *Jackanapes.* In the eighteen-eighties, Fredericton was the home not only of the three writing Roberts that we have mentioned but also of the poets Bliss Carman, Francis Sherman, and Barry Straton. In the early years of this century, Fredericton had to be content to be known as the birth-place of writers who were no longer in residence, but in the nineteen-twenties a new literary generation developed: Dorothy Roberts wrote her early poetry there, her father Theodore returned to live there (he was still living there in 1944 when I first went to Fredericton), and Alfred Bailey and Malcolm Ross began to write their poetry and prose while students at the university. The literary tradition of Fredericton has continued up to the present. In 1945 Alfred Bailey and others founded *The Fiddlehead,* a magazine of verse which is still flourishing and in which a group of new young poets, including Elizabeth Brewster, Fred Cogswell, Robert Rogers and, most recently, Alden Nowlan, published most of their early work. In 1952, Brigadier Michael Wardell, an associate of Lord Beaverbrook, established in Fredericton the University Press of New Brunswick, and he has published a number of books by local authors and others and has established a magazine, *The Atlantic Advocate,* which is doing much to enrich the cultural and political life of the Atlantic Provinces. It has been said that there are more poets per square mile in Fredericton than in any other area of Canada, and I can well believe it. It is interesting to note that in his introduction to *Writing in Canada,* the report of the Canadian Writers' Conference held at Kingston in 1955, F. R. Scott was able truthfully to say "with few exceptions, the writers all came from the five cities of Vancouver, Toronto, Kingston, Montreal, and Fredericton." To be included in this list may not have meant much to the metropolises of Toronto and Montreal, but it meant a great deal to the comparatively tiny city of Fredericton! And it provided external authority for my claim that in Fredericton at least the Roberts tradition is a living one.

That Roberts was conscious of the literary tradition of Fredericton is clear from an essay on that city by him which I recently found in typescript in the U.N.B. library. So far as I know, this essay was never published in his lifetime. (It did appear, however, in the February, 1961 issue of *The Atlantic Advocate.*) In it Roberts mentions Juliana Horatia Ewing and declares that Fredericton "intellectually and socially wields an influence out of all proportion to her size." But what this essay chiefly reveals is Roberts' keen awareness of the physical beauty of Fredericton. He writes in part as follows:

Fredericton lies on a point of deep-soiled intervale, eighty-four miles above the mouth of the river Saint John. About her the great river draws a broad and gleaming crescent. Behind her rises a rampart of wooded hills. Opposite to her wharves flow in two lovely tributary streams, the Nashwaak and the Nashwaaksis, offering ceaseless enticement to the lovers of birch and paddle. And into the Nashwaak itself, just above the bridge that spans its mouth, empties a lilied, slow-winding, greenly shadowed brook, dear to those who go canoeing just two in a canoe. This is fitly known as "Lovers' Creek." ... A little above the city the river is thickly sown with islands, level and grassy, enringed with trees, and holding out the most tempting invitations to all who would go camping.

Undoubtedly the sheer physical beauty of Fredericton did much to inspire the poetry of Roberts, Carman, and their friends. As A. J. M. Smith has put it, in the Founders' Day Address which he gave at the University of New Brunswick in 1946, "The Fredericton of the seventies ... appears like an enchanted city, with its elm-shaded streets, its generously proportioned old homes, its Cathedral, and the college on the hill, while the river winding through the town and the wooded slopes behind bring the forests and an echo of the sea almost to people's very doorsteps."

But there was a quality in the social life of Fredericton which also put its stamp upon Charles Roberts. Settled first by United Empire Loyalists, Fredericton retained in the days of Roberts, and indeed retains to this day, many of their values and attitudes. Some, if not all, of these values were admirable. From the very first, the Loyalists showed their interest in education by the early establishment of the College of New Brunswick, and this interest in culture and the things of the mind gave to Fredericton an intellectual quality rare indeed in a pioneer country. The Loyalist founders stood, also, for the values which we associate with the aristocratic tradition: they vowed to make the infant province of New Brunswick "the most gentlemanly on earth," and they clung tenaciously to courtesy, gentility, and good breeding in their social relationships. The social life which revolved about the Cathedral, Government House, the Garrison, the University, and the Legislative Assembly reminds us rather of that of Bath or of some other eighteenth-century resort of fashion than of a pioneer community surrounded by untracked forests. First-hand testimony of this is provided by Sir George Parkin (of whom more later) who in 1920 wrote, in a letter to Dr. L. W. Bailey which Sir John Willison quotes in his book on Parkin: "My wife and I often speak of the immense advantage we gained from living in such surroundings as we had in the Fredericton of our early days. There was an old-fashioned courtesy and dignity, a real interest in the things of the mind and spirit, which seem to have somewhat disappeared in the rush of life and supposed progress of later times." As one who is proud to call Fredericton his adopted home, I should like to say that I do not believe this atmosphere has been altogether lost. I encountered it the moment I arrived in Fredericton, and have cherished it ever since: gentleness, courtesy, a genuine respect for learning and literature.

Now all this left a deep mark on Roberts. In the autobiographical notes to which I referred earlier, Roberts wrote under the heading of "purpose": "to write good literature, but underlying it to make for chivalry." In all his work we see evidence of the chivalric values: through it all shine his dignity, restraint, compassion, courtesy, and courage. I never met Sir Charles Roberts, but I did come to know his younger brother Theodore well, and at the risk of sounding dreadfully old-fashioned I am prepared to say that Theodore Roberts was every inch a gentleman. His tall, erect figure, his soft but pleasing voice, his grace of manner, his complete absence of pomposity, his readiness to encourage a young writer, his unfailing gentleness and courtesy: these I shall always remember as embodying at its best the social tradition of Fredericton. Again I say the tradition is a living one, for almost all the same qualities are exhibited by Theodore's son, the painter Goodridge Roberts.

I feel that at this point I may be in danger of sentimentality, of exaggerating the good qualities of the city which has sometimes sarcastically been called "The Celestial City." Let me, then, by way of light relief if nothing else, quote two less flattering references to Fredericton. The first is a glimpse of the city as it was when Roberts was still in residence, and comes from the pen of an anonymous U.N.B. undergraduate writing in the *University Monthly* in March, 1882. After paying Fredericton a number of compliments, he went on, "Its streets are well laid out, but its sidewalks are either not up to the standard or else entirely wanting. . . . The water in Fredericton, for the most part, is not fit to drink, and the sooner means are devised and arrangements made for the supply of better water to the city, the sooner will Fredericton rise from its present lethargic state to an active and live town." Civic pride urges me to point out that Fredericton now has an excellent water system! The other unflattering reference is much more recent, and comes from the pen of the young Toronto poet, Raymond Souster:

> Fredericton
> So this is "the poets' corner
> Of Canada" — Bliss, Sir Charles,
> And Francis Joseph Sherman,
> All born, all Latin'd and Greek'd here.
>
> Not one of them
> With anything really to say,

But dressing it up, faking it,
So that they fooled quite a few in their time.

And I can understand why.
Outside of the noble river
Which none of them bothered to write about,
This city has little to commend it,
And couldn't help but in time
Drive a man to drink or lousy poetry.

Which vices are no doubt being practised
At this very moment today.

Well, I like Souster's poems very much when they are poking fun at his native Toronto, but I must say that he shows a remarkable inability to see the true nature of Fredericton!

From the civic tradition I turn now to the academic tradition of Roberts. It is in this connection that native and adopted sons of New Brunswick feel that least justice has been done to them by Upper Canadians. In his *Colony to Nation,* Professor A. R. M. Lower let fall the unfortunate remark that "curiously enough it was the sterile soil of New Brunswick which bred the Roberts family and their relative Bliss Carman"; Elsie Pomeroy in her biography of Roberts dismisses his school and university years with a tribute to Parkin and a few anecdotes; and Professor Pelham Edgar, in the article to which I referred at the beginning of this paper, expressed what we may call the orthodox Toronto sneer most explicitly when he wrote, "Of the formal education received both at the collegiate school, and during his three years (1876-1879) at the University of New Brunswick, there is not a great deal to be said. The staffs were not noteworthy in the scholarly sense, and we may assume that the standards were not, on a comparative estimate, high." The most succinct and accurate comment on that is unprintable: but to put it politely, nothing could be further from the truth.

There are actually three New Brunswick institutions of learning which can legitimately claim some significant part in the moulding of Charles Roberts: Mount Allison University, the Fredericton Collegiate School, and the University of New Brunswick. Mount Allison's part was a small but nevertheless a significant one: when Roberts' father was rector of Westcock, Charles showed a juvenile talent for painting, and arrangements were made for the boy to take classes at Mount Allison from Professor Gray. From these classes, I presume, we may trace the very strong sense of design which is such a conspicuous feature of Roberts' descriptive poems. At the Fredericton Collegiate School, of which his grandfather had been so long the headmaster, and which had and has for generations been the chief feeder of the University, Roberts had the good fortune to come under the influence of George R. (later Sir George) Parkin.

So much has been said of Parkin's influence upon Roberts and Carman that I do not need to dwell upon it here. Parkin was himself a graduate of the University of New Brunswick, getting his degree in the year of Confederation, and in an autobiographical fragment he thus described the education he received there in the sixties:

Our President, Brydone-Jack, trained in the severe school of the Scottish universities, taught us mathematics; Montgomery-Campbell, fresh from his fellowship at a Cambridge college, brought us the inspiration and culture of an ancient English university; Professor Bailey, a student under Agassiz at Harvard, filled us with the enthusiasm for natural science which he had caught from his famous master; Baron d'Avray, a Jerseyman of French descent, with all the delicate courtesy of his race, combined a refined taste in English literature with a perfect mastery of French. Three years of work spent under such able and inspiring teachers went far to remedy the worst defects of earlier education and at least opened the doors for wider knowledge.

(In Willison, *Sir George Parkin*)

In 1871 Parkin was appointed headmaster of the Collegiate School upon the resignation of Roberts' grandfather, but after two years he obtained leave of absence and spent the year 1873-4 in Oxford. At Oxford Parkin listened to Ruskin's lectures on art, to Dean Stanley's sermons on liberal theology, to T. H. Green's lectures on philosophy and Bonamy Price's lectures on political economy; he read the new poetry of Tennyson, Rossetti, Arnold, and Swinburne; and he was elected Secretary of the Oxford Union, an almost unique honour for a freshman. It was a Parkin fresh from such exciting experiences that Roberts and Carman had as their teacher—no wonder that Carman called him "a fascinating teacher, this intense and magnetic personality." Carman goes on:

"I don't remember that my lessons in the old school were ever drudg-

40

ery. Often we would not cover more than a few lines in the hour. A reference might occur which would bring up a side issue in history or mythology, and then we must see how some modern or contemporary writer had treated the same theme. One of the class would be sent running to Parkin's rooms to fetch a book. Tennyson, perhaps, or Rossetti, or Arnold, or another, and we must listen to his poem on the subject. These were wonderful hours of growth, though we never dreamed of our incomparable good fortune. . . ."

(In Willison, *Sir George Parkin*)

Parkin, of course, went on to greater things—to the principalship of Upper Canada College, the secretaryship of the Rhodes Trust, and to the authorship of several books of history and biography—but it is doubtful if he did anything more permanently valuable than stimulate the youthful imaginations of Roberts and Carman.

But Parkin's great influence upon them has, somewhat unfairly, overshadowed the influence of the professors at the University of New Brunswick to which, in due course, the poets passed. That university, projected as far back as 1785 by the Loyalist founders of the province, had struggled along for almost a century when Roberts entered it. Although it was still a small university, it had weathered its worst storms in the eighteen-fifties, and, following its reorganization as the secular provincial university in 1859, it had begun to move steadily forward. That its standards were not low, as the late Dr. Edgar would have it, is attested by the brilliant series of graduates who emerged from it in the sixties, seventies, and eighties—men such as James F. McCurdy, for many years Professor of Oriental Literature in the University of Toronto, James Mitchell and William Pugsley, both of whom became Premiers of New Brunswick, George E. Foster, a member of the Federal Cabinet for over twenty years, Archdeacon W.O. Raymond, clergyman and scholarly historian, John Douglas Hazen, later premier of New Brunswick and Minister of Marine and Fisheries in the Federal cabinet, and Walter C. Murray, who became the first president of the University of Saskatchewan. Another proof of the university's vitality in these years is the outstanding record of its seniors in the examinations for the Gilchrist Scholarship, and by the success of its graduates in winning prizes at Oxford, Edinburgh, Harvard, and other great centres of learning.

Fortunately, we have first-hand testimony of the influence the little university exercised upon its students. I have already quoted Parkin's testimony. Here is what his class-mate, George E. Foster (later Sir George Foster) said of its influence upon him:

On the whole, I incline to the opinion that the course of training received was quite as beneficial to the undergraduates as would have been possible at one of the larger universities. Under its ministry I pursued my way from the preliminary instruction of the school to a wider and ever-widening field of knowledge in Classics and Mathematics, of both of which I was fond, and of Natural Science, a hitherto unknown field in which I found especial attractions.... The grounding and stimulus received at my Alma Mater I can trace through my whole life as a resourceful and sustaining foundation.
(W. Stewart Wallace, *The Memoirs of the Rt. Hon. Sir George Foster*)

Most fortunately, I am able to give you a first-hand account of Roberts' own sense of debt to the University of New Brunswick. For the first time I discovered recently in our library archives a signed typescript of a talk on U.N.B. in the 1870's given by Sir Charles himself on February 5, 1942. Since I do not think the talk has ever previously been published, I shall give it in full:

Looking back across the years I realize ever more and more clearly that, for my temperament at least, it was a great piece of good fortune to have been educated at what was then a small college, the University of New Brunswick, — a small college, indeed, but one with a definite atmosphere of its own and a distinctly formative tradition. The handful of Freshmen who gathered each September on the Terrace and eyed each other with suspicious curiosity consisted for the most part of more or less raw material, somewhat leavened by four or five youthful matriculants from the Collegiate or High School of Fredericton, Saint John or Saint Stephen. These were speedily drawn under the influence of a very attenuated staff—a president and four professors each responsible for several subjects of the curriculum. This influence, exerted unconsciously but all the more potently for that, and accepted with equal unconsciousness by its recipients, worked upon us with remarkable efficiency, so that long before the year was out these very "verdant" Freshmen had all insensibly taken on the College stamp. In my own case, as I remember, we were an unruly and turbulent class, not easy to assimilate; but it soon came about, somehow, that unsuspectingly we were ruled, and liked it. In the true sense of the word we were being educated, rather than merely lectured at.

42

We were being securely grounded in fundamental things, and we were being specialized not at all. At the end of our course we found ourselves prepared to choose understandingly our own individual careers and with some confidence to embark upon them. . . .

My own personal debt to this small college that then was is incalculable. It confirmed and increased that love for Greek and Latin literature which had been first inspired by my father in private lessons and later nourished by Dr. Bridges and Dr. Parkin at the Collegiate School of Fredericton. Greek, Latin and English Literature (but Homer and Milton especially) were the formative influences to which I have chiefly owed whatever there may be of excellence, if any, in my own literary output. In the intimate teaching of this small college stress was laid upon the beauty and wisdom of these literatures rather than upon the dry bones of grammar and rhetoric which, of necessity, underlay them. In other words, the teaching I received was inspirational before it was mechanical.

In these few lines I am paying grateful tribute not by any means to the small colleges in general but to this small college as I experienced it. And my appreciation of this small college that was does not in the least conflict with my admiration of, and my unbounded aspiration for, the great and distinguished University which it is coming to be.

Who were the "president and four professors" to whom Roberts refers? The president was still William Brydone Jack, professor of Mathematics, Natural Philosophy, and Astronomy. Jack, a native of Dumfriesshire, had such a brilliant record in mathematics and physics at St. Andrew's that, on his graduation as Master of Arts in 1840, he was offered the professorship of physics at New College, Manchester, as successor to the great physicist, Dr. John Dalton. He chose rather to come to the tiny King's College, Fredericton, where he lectured for forty-five years and from 1861 to 1885 served as president. He was especially interested in astronomy, and was among the first to make use of telegraphy in determining longitude. His work in this connection was of great service to Sir William Logan in his construction of the geological map of Canada.

The professor of Chemistry and Natural Science was Loring Woart Bailey, grandfather of the present Dean of Arts at U.N.B., Dr. Alfred G. Bailey. Loring Bailey was a member of the famous class of '59 at Harvard, and had Charles W. Eliot as his tutor in mathematics, Louis Agassiz as his instructor in biology, and Long-fellow as his professor of modern literature. After graduating from Harvard, Bailey was appointed as assistant in the Department of Chemistry under Professor Josiah P. Cooke; and from Harvard he came directly to Fredericton, where he remained for over half a century. In his lifetime he published scores of scientific papers, and he was at various times offered professorships at Bowdoin, Colby, Vassar, and McGill.

The professor of English Language and Literature and Mental and Moral Philosophy in Roberts' time was Thomas Harrison. Harrison was a native of Sheffield, New Brunswick, who for some reason had passed up the nearby provincial university to attend Trinity College, Dublin. There he compiled a brilliant academic record, graduating with honours in Mathematics and Natural Philosophy. When in 1885 he succeeded Jack in the presidency of U.N.B., Harrison took over the lecturing in Mathematics. Of his ability to teach English we know nothing directly; we can only guess that it was of a high order from this comment in the *University Monthly* of February, 1883: "The *Argosy* [the student newspaper of Mount Allison University] contains an article against the want of an English course at Sackville. If the students of Sackville attain their object they will look back upon the days spent in the study of English literature as among the most interesting and most profitable of their college course. It is the study above all others in the University of New Brunswick in which students take an interest. In this department more students find an incentive to study than in any other branch of the course."

The professor of Classical Literature and History was George Eulas Foster, to whom I have already referred. Another native of New Brunswick, he graduated from the provincial university in 1867, taught school for a few years, and in 1872-3 studied at Edinburgh and Heidelberg. At Edinburgh he had Sellar as his professor of Latin, Blackie as his professor of Greek, and Masson as his professor of English. Under Masson he won a much-coveted prize in English literature. In September, 1873, Foster returned to Fredericton as professor of classics in the University of New Brunswick. He was soon greatly in demand as a public lecturer, and his skill in this respect took him, after six years, into politics. For over twenty years he was a member of the Federal Cabinet;

he was on several occasions acting Prime Minister of Canada; he was Canada's representative at the Peace Conference and at the League of Nations; and his reputation for oratory was such that he was frequently called "the Demosthenes of Canada."

Of the fourth professor, Francis Philibert Rivet, professor of French Language and Literature, I have been able to discover nothing. But what I have said of the four men above indicates beyond serious doubt, I believe, that the professors under whom Roberts studied at the University of New Brunswick were scholars of real distinction. They represented between them the universities of St. Andrew's, Trinity College, Dublin, Harvard, Heidelberg, and Edinburgh, and at all these great international centres of learning they had acquitted themselves brilliantly. They served a small provincial university, but they were far from being provincial mediocrities themselves. *The University Monthly* was probably quite correct when, in April, 1885, replying to charges of weakness made by Toronto's *Varsity*, it stated flatly, "A more capable staff of instructors is not to be found in any other institution of a like nature in Canada."

Before leaving this subject of Roberts' academic tradition, I should like to point out that the Roberts tradition at the University of New Brunswick is still very much alive. All of his books, and many of his letters and manuscripts, are preserved in the University Library; his works have been the subject of two M.A. theses in recent years; his portrait hangs in the reading-room of the library and was the subject of a recent poem by Elizabeth Brewster; a monument to Roberts, Carman, and Sherman stands on the campus in front of the old Arts Building; and there was recently established the Roberts Prize for the best short story submitted each year by a student of the university; and his nephew, Goodridge Roberts, was the resident artist at the university in 1959–60.

In June of 1883 Charles G. D. Roberts, a young man of only twenty-three, delivered the Alumni Oration at his alma mater. His title was "The Beginnings of Canadian Literature," and the few names he was able to educe—Charles Heavysege, John Hunter-Duvar, C. P. Mulvany, "Fidelis" and "Seranus" in poetry for example—are evidence of the virtual vacuum which he had set himself to fill. In assessing Roberts' place in the national tradition, it is only proper to remind ourselves that when he came on the scene he was virtually alone. Roberts' contemporaries were aware of this. Archibald Lampman wrote:

Almost all the verse-writing published in Canada before the appearance of *Orion* was of a more or less barbarous character. The drama of *Saul* by Charles Heavysege and some of Heavysege's sonnets are about the only exceptions which can be made to this statement. Mr. Roberts was the first Canadian writer in verse who united a strong original genius with a high degree of culture and an acute literary judgment. He was the first to produce a style strongly individual in tone, and founded on the study of the best writers.

(University of Toronto Quarterly, 1944)

There is no denying Roberts' importance in our literary history. He it was above all others who started the Group of the Sixties and within a decade of the date of his Alumni Oration made Canadian poetry known and respected throughout the English-speaking world.

By saying this I do not mean to imply that Roberts was better than Carman, or Lampman, or Scott. I deprecate all attempts to rank these four poets. There was no rivalry between them: in all the letters and critical articles of the four that I have read I have never found the slightest evidence of jealousy among them. They all agreed that Roberts was their leader, in the sense that he first published his poems in the great magazines of North America and in book form, but he was the first among equals. We must, I think, consider the Confederation Group as a group, noting differences between them, but not seeking to select one or two as "masters" and discussing the others as also-rans. All four of them had in common the great distinction that, in contrast with all the colonial versifiers who had preceded them, they looked clearsightedly at the Canadian landscape and the Canadian people. They shared the further distinction that they took the craft of poetry seriously. They all wrote a quantity of mediocre verse, but they all wrote a few poems which were as different from the verse of Sangster and Mair and Hunter-Duvar as chalk is from cheese. To suggest, as some recent critics have, that anthologies of Canadian verse should virtually begin with Dr. Pratt is absurd. I yield to no one in my admiration for Dr. Pratt, but to begin the study of Canadian poetry with him would be to ignore some of the finest poems we have yet produced or are likely to produce for many decades. Surely only prejudice or ignorance could lead anyone seriously to assert that we should jettison Carman's "Low Tide on Grand Pré," Duncan Campbell Scott's "The Piper of Arll," Lampman's "Heat," or Roberts' "Tantramar Revisited."

In calling this group the Confederation Poets, as Malcolm Ross has done in his recent, admirable selection of their work in the New Canadian Library, we are drawing attention to an important part of their inspiration: the new national feeling that resulted from the union of the provinces in 1867. As a boy, Roberts derived a sense of national pride from his father. Miss Pomeroy tells us:

From the first suggestion of Confederation his father had been an ardent supporter of the idea, and had talked about it to his young son. Never did the boy forget his father's enthusiasm when the Union was about to be achieved. Standing out clearly in his mind was a drive through the Dorchester Woods in the early summer of 1867, when his father expatiated on the great event of that time, dwelling particularly upon the leaders' vision which was responsible for the Union, and upon their faith in its ultimate outcome, a great united Canada "which would stretch from sea to sea." Soon Dorchester Church came into view, but before dismissing the subject, the Rector added, "In the building of this young nation I hope my son will grow up to play his full part."

Charles Roberts never lost this sense of national purpose. In his Alumni Oration he urged upon the university a more conscious concern with Canadian life and Canadian literature: "Where do we want a more vivid realization of the fact that we have a country, and are making a nation; that we have a history, and are making a literature; that we have a heroic past, and are making ready for a future that shall not be inglorious? In our universities, if they would not lose their birthright." His poem "Canada" expresses, if somewhat too rhetorically, his faith in Canada's destiny, and his *History of Canada* is full of pride in Canada's past and of high hopes for Canada's future.

But the most permanently valuable expressions of Roberts' love of country were not these direct ones, but the stories and above all the poems in which this love was given indirect expression. This brings us, rather belatedly perhaps, to Roberts' actual writings. We have seen the traditions that shaped him—a scholarly family,

47

a beautiful city and province, a group of inspired teachers, an outburst of national excitement. Now we must ask whether the results of all these influences were of any permanent value.

Of Roberts' prose, I do not intend to say much. Roberts himself said that he lived *by* prose *for* poetry, and there is in his prose a commercial, journalistic quality that is quite lacking from the best of his verse. His *History of Canada* (1897) has an excellent treatment of the early part of our story, an adequate account of the early nineteenth century, a scrappy and desultory account of the decades after Confederation, and a somewhat rhetorical conclusion in which Roberts weighs the respective advantages of Annexation, Independence, and Imperial Federation and comes out in favour of the last. I could not conscientiously recommend anyone to read the whole book today, rather than, say, the histories of Creighton and Lower, but I do think that some of his descriptions of early episodes in our history might be included in school textbooks. Indeed, there is a certain juvenile quality about most of Roberts' prose. His historical novels, such as *The Forge in the Forest* (1896), *A Sister to Evangeline* (1898), *Barbara Ladd* (1902), and *The Prisoner of Mademoiselle* (1904), are costume melodramas that might still enliven the imaginations of teen-age boys, but have little appeal to the mature reader. Even his more serious novels, such as *The Heart of the Ancient Wood* (1900) and *In the Morning of Time* (1919), which were Roberts' own favourites and were declared by Pelham Edgar to be of "enduring fascination," seem merely quaint today.

Only the short stories among his prose, I believe, have any chance of permanent survival. And even here, we must eliminate all those stories which deal with human, as distinct from animal, life. The stories of human life that cause one to hesitate before dismissing them—such, for example, as "The Perdu" or "The Black-water Pot"—make their claim to attention by their accuracy and suggestiveness of natural description; but their characters are so stereotyped, so one-dimensional, that, rather reluctantly, one has to discard them. Roberts had literally no power of creating credible human beings. In the best of the animal stories, however, this weakness is not apparent, and here the brilliantly accurate descriptions and compelling atmospheric effects are sufficient. Stories such as " 'The Young Ravens That Call upon Him' " and

48

"The Heron in the Reeds" have a kind of classic simplicity which makes them, within their admittedly narrow limits, virtually invulnerable. " 'The Young Ravens That Call upon Him' " especially, with its camera-eye technique, its subtlety of atmospheric detail, its structural juxtaposition of eagle and ewe, and its constant restraint of utterance, strikes me as a classic. The final two paragraphs, in which the contentment of the eagles is contrasted with the agony of the ewe whose lamb the eagle has snatched away, are worthy of reading as an example of what Roberts could do in stories of this sort:

In the nest of the eagles there was content. The pain of their hunger appeased, the nestlings lay dozing in the sun, the neck of one resting across the back of the other. The triumphant male sat erect upon his perch, staring out over the splendid world that displayed itself beneath him. Now and again he half lifted his wings and screamed joyously at the sun. The mother bird, perched upon a limb on the edge of the nest, busily rearranged her plumage. At times she stooped her head into the nest to utter over her sleeping eaglets a soft chuckling noise, which seemed to come from the bottom of her throat.

But hither and thither over the round bleak hill wandered the ewe, calling for her lamb, unmindful of the flock, which had been moved to other pastures.

What really captures our interest in these animal stories, apart from their realistic portrayal of the cruelty and terror which dominate the natural world, is their accuracy of observation and their strong sense of design. These, too, are the best qualities of Roberts' poetry. Much nonsense has been talked about "mere nature description" in poetry, as if anyone with the time and the will could write it. The fact is that really to see a scene, and still more the ability clearly to record one's observations, is a very rare capacity indeed. Most of us go through life with our eyes half closed, and it is the poet and the painter who do our seeing for us. Even poets, as a reading of Goldsmith, Sangster, and Mair will indicate, have a tendency to see a scene through the eyes of other poets, rather than through their own. When Roberts' "Tantramar Revisited" appeared in *The Week* in 1883, it was the first poem published in Canada to see a part of the Canadian landscape as it really was:

Skirting the sunbright uplands stretches a riband of meadow,

49

Shorn of the labouring grass, bulwarked well from the sea,
Fenced on its seaward border with long clay dikes from the turbid
Surge and flow of the tides vexing the Westmoreland shores.
Yonder, toward the left, lie broad the Westmoreland marshes,—
Miles on miles they extend, level, and grassy, and dim,
Clear from the long red sweep of flats to the sky in the distance,
Save for the outlying heights, green-rampired Cumberland Point;
Miles on miles outrolled, and the river-channels divide them,—
Miles on miles of green, barred by the hurtling gusts.

Miles on miles beyond the tawny bay is Minudie,
There are the low blue hills; villages gleam at their feet.
Nearer a white sail shines across the water, and nearer
Still are the slim, grey masts of fishing boats dry on the flats.
Ah, how well I remember those wide red flats, above tide-mark,
Pale with scurf of the salt, seamed and baked in the sun!
Well I remember the piles of blocks and ropes, and the net-reels
Wound with the beaded nets, dripping and dark from the sea!
Now at this season the nets are unwound; they hang from the rafters
Over the fresh-stowed hay in upland barns, and the wind
Blows all day through the chinks, with the streaks of sunlight, and
    sways them
Softly at will; or they lie heaped in the gloom of a loft.

That is descriptive poetry of a high order. The epithets are not
the conventional "verdants" and "pensives" of Sangster, but each
has been chosen deliberately to suggest the exact nature of the
scene before the poet's eyes. "Labouring," for example, is calculated exactly to summon up the picture of that long marsh grass
of the Tantramar country, which is constantly in slow, troubled
motion from the winds that blow off the bay. "Turbid" catches
exactly the twisting muddy tumult of the incoming Fundy tide,
stirring up the red mud of the flats and river channels. "Barred
by the hurtling gusts" was a phrase the accuracy of which I did
not appreciate until I had seen the Tantramar marshes and the
peculiar way in which gusts of wind, by bending the grasses over
in parallel strips, do cause a series of darker bars of colour to
move over the meadows.

But of course it is not merely the accuracy of the individual
details that distinguishes this poem. There is also the way in which
these details are arranged into a series of patterns or designs, and
these designs in turn into the structure of the whole poem. The

poem begins with a reference to the poet's own losses at the hands
of time, and then turns to the Tantramar, which he declares to
be unchanged. He then describes the Tantramar scene from his
vantage point on a hill-top, beginning with the road that leads
down to the plains beside the sea, the houses and orchards that
dot them, the marshes that extend along the edge of the bay, and
on to the distant blue hills on the far shore: leading one's eye
from the near scene to the far horizon. Then he begins to reverse
the process: the white sail brings us back across the bay, the
fishing-boats and nets bring us back to the mud flats at the
water's edge, fresh-stowed hay suggests the meadows and the
farms, and so on. Finally, he completes the design by bringing our
attention back to himself, and his awareness that even here, if he
looked closely, he would find the hands of chance and change at
work.

Another distinctive element in the poem is its metrical ingenuity.
The poem is written in the classical elegiac metre, in alternate
dactylic hexameters and pentameters, which had been recently
employed by Clough, Arnold, and Longfellow. It was probably
Longfellow's *Evangeline* that provided Roberts with his metrical
model, but the charge of derivativeness has little weight if, as I
believe is the case here, the imitation surpasses the model. Here
are a few lines from *Evangeline:*

Far in the West there lies a desert land, where the mountains
Lift, through perpetual snows, their lofty and luminous summits.
Down from their jagged, deep ravines, where the gorge, like a gateway,
Opens a passage rude to the wheels of the emigrant's wagon,
Westward the Oregon flows and the Walleway and Owyhee.
Eastward, with devious course, among the Wind-river Mountains,
Through the Sweet-water Valley precipitate leaps the Nebraska.

Surely these lines are relatively clumsy and cumbrous and monot-
onous. They show little of Roberts' power to modulate the movement of the rhythm to suit the material with which he is dealing.
Notice, for example, how Roberts, in the passage I have already
quoted, uses the first long, unpunctuated line, "Skirting the sunbright uplands stretches a riband of meadow," with its repeated
r's and its short vowels, to suggest length and light, and then
breaks the next line, "Shorn of the labouring grass, bulwarked
well from the sea," in half to give, first, the effect of the short,

clipped grass and, second, the effect of the dike blocking the sea. The music and rhythm of Roberts' poem has a quality which is all his own. It is not the cumbrous, sing-song music of Longfellow, nor the soft, sad, austere music of Arnold, nor the lilting melody of Carman, nor the slow, wistful, meditative music of much of Lampman: it is a grave, masculine, striding song, a trifle heavy perhaps, at moments a little bit too deliberate, but on the whole striking a very happy balance between over-facility and awkwardness. A more facile rhythm would have been quite inappropriate to the somewhat harsh and forbidding Tantramar country, a more hesitant one would not have captured the flow of wind over grass and sea.

Many of the qualities found in "Tantramar Revisited" occur again in the best of Roberts' sonnets. Here, for example, is "The Potato Harvest":

> A high bare field, brown from the plough, and borne
>   Aslant from sunset; amber wastes of sky
>   Washing the ridge; a clamour of crows that fly
> In from the wide flats where the spent tides mourn
> To yon their rocking roosts in pines wind-torn;
>   A line of grey snake-fence, that zigzags by
>   A pond and cattle; from the homestead nigh
> The long deep summonings of the supper horn.
>
> Black on the ridge, against that lonely flush,
>   A cart, and stoop-necked oxen; ranged beside,
>   Some barrels; and the day-worn harvest-folk,
> Here, emptying their baskets, jar the hush
>   With hollow thunders. Down the dusk hillside
>   Lumbers the wain; and day fades out like smoke.

In that sonnet the painterly quality in Roberts is very evident: the colours are all exactly specified, and the eye is led from the hill and sky by the crows and the snake-fence to the farmstead in the octave, and again from the hill to the house by the wagon in the sestet. The whole picture has the clarity and homely charm of a Breughel, together with Breughel's strength and firmness of structure. But complementing the pictorial pattern is a pattern of sounds: the clamour of the crows, the mourn of the tides, and the comforting call of the supper horn in the octave are balanced by the thunder of the potatoes into the barrels and the lumbering noise of the homecoming wagon in the sestet. A moment of activity has been fully captured; and the sense of the completion of a cycle is suggested by the beautiful closing phrase, "and day fades out like smoke."

There are a dozen such sonnets in which Roberts catches with loving and yet quite unsentimental fidelity the rural life and landscape of the Maritime Provinces. Most of them are to be found in what is undoubtedly his finest volume, *Songs of the Common Day* (1893). In that volume he had the happy inspiration of recording in a sonnet sequence the procession of the seasons in his native environment. One wonders what source those critics who dismiss Roberts' poetry as completely derivative would educe for this sonnet sequence. Sonnet sequences aplenty were found in Elizabethan England, and Rossetti's *The House of Life* provided a more recent example; but these sonnet sequences dealt with love, not with the humble occupations of everyday life. The idea of the celebration of rustic life probably came to him from Virgil, but the idea of celebrating it in a series of sonnets seems to have been original.

I am so fond of Roberts' sonnets of everyday life that I am tempted to linger over them. In justice to him, however, I must draw your attention to others of his poems which I feel deserve a place in our living tradition. He wrote in "Marsyas" a fine poem on a classical theme, and in "Grey Rocks and Greyer Sea," "Epitaph for a Sailor Buried Ashore," "Epitaph for a Husbandman," and above all in "Ave," a group of moving elegies. The elegy, with its quiet dignity of tone, was peculiarly well suited to Roberts' talent. I am less fond of his mystical poems, which have been widely praised but which seem to me vague and rhetorical. "In the Wide Awe and Wisdom of the Night" is probably the best of them, and even it concludes with a rhetorical flourish which is more remarkable for its sound than its sense:

> And knew the Universe of no such span
> As the august infinitude of Man.

I do not think that Roberts' directly patriotic poems will survive either: one can admire their sincerity, admit that they once played their part in stimulating a slowly developing sense of Canadian nationhood, and yet believe that they are too pontifical, too solemnly vainglorious, to suit the modern temper. I should prefer, before concluding, to quote one or two relatively unknown poems by Roberts that seem to me to have qualities worth preserving. "The Brook in February" has a child-like innocence which I find much more attractive than Roberts' more pretentious philosophical and political verses:

> A snowy path for squirrel and fox,
>   It winds between the wintry firs.
> Snow-muffled are its iron rocks,
>   And o'er its stillness nothing stirs.
>
> But low, bend low a listening ear!
>   Beneath the mask of moveless white
> A babbling whisper you shall hear—
>   Of birds and blossoms, leaves and light.

"Monition," in contrast, is a deft little poem of warning, and evokes very briefly and suggestively a sense of doom:

> A faint wind, blowing from World's End,
>   Made strange the city street.
> A strange sound mingled in the fall
>   Of the familiar feet.
>
> Something unseen whirled with the leaves
>   To tap on door and sill.
> Something unknown went whispering by
>   Even when the wind was still.
>
> And men looked up with startled eyes
>   And hurried on their way,
> As if they had been called, and told
>   How brief their day.

There is not time for "The Iceberg," the minor masterpiece of Roberts' later life, but I can find a moment for one of my own favourites, "Philander's Song," which reminds us that Roberts at heart was not a solemn man, for all his sense of dedication, but a gay lover of life and love:

> I sat and read Anacreon,
>   Moved by the gay, delicious measure
> I mused that lips were made for love,
>   And love to charm a poet's leisure.

And as I mused a maid came by
With something in her look that caught me.
Forgotten was Anacreon's line,
But not the lesson he had taught me.

It was almost exactly seventy years ago, on the evening of February 19, 1891, in a public lecture in this city of Ottawa, that Archibald Lampman paid his personal tribute to Roberts' influence. It is a famous and oft-quoted passage, but the coincidence of time and circumstance emboldens me to quote it yet again:

As regards Mr. Roberts' work, I have always had a personal feeling which perhaps induces me to place a higher estimate upon it in some respects than my hearers will care to accept. To most younger Canadians who are interested in literature, especially those who have written themselves, Mr. Roberts occupies a peculiar position. They are accustomed to look up to him as in some sort the founder of a school, the originator of a new era in our poetic activity. I hope my hearers will pardon me, if I go out of my way to illustrate this fact by describing the effect Mr. Roberts' poems produced upon me when I first met with them.

It was almost ten years ago, and I was very young, an undergraduate at college. One May evening somebody lent me *Orion and Other Poems,* then recently published. Like most of the young fellows about me, I had been under the depressing conviction that we were situated hopelessly on the outskirts of civilization, where no art and no literature could be, and that it was useless to expect that anything great could be done by any of our companions, still more useless to expect that we could do it ourselves. I sat up most of the night reading and re-reading *Orion* in a state of the wildest excitement and when I went to bed I could not sleep. It seemed to me a wonderful thing that such work could be done by a Canadian, by a young man, one of ourselves. It was like a voice from some new paradise of art, calling to us to be up and doing. A little after sunrise I got up and went out into the college grounds. The air, I remember, was full of the odour and cool sunshine of the spring morning. The dew was thick upon the grass. All the birds of our Maytime seemed to be singing in the oaks, and there were even a few adder-tongues and trilliums still blooming on the slope of the little ravine. But everything was transfigured for me beyond description, bathed in an old-world radiance of beauty [by] the magic of the lines that were sounding in my ears, those divine verses, as they seemed to me, with their Tennyson-like richness and strange, earth-loving, Greekish flavour. I have never forgotten that morning, and its influence has always remained with me.

(*University of Toronto Quarterly*, 1944)

Fifty years after Lampman made this acknowledgement, Professor Pelham Edgar wrote:

The future will recognize even more than we are willing to do that Roberts was a pivotal figure, a musical hinge around which our poetry first began to revolve. Our younger poets of today may not recognize their debt, for it is the time-honoured privilege of youth to repudiate its own ancestry and overleap the generations; but in the long perspective of history the pervasive quality of Roberts' influence will be recognized at its true importance.

(*University of Toronto Quarterly*, 1943)

For my own part, I place myself with Lampman and Edgar rather than with those more recent critics who would consign Roberts to the New Brunswick Museum. The type of poetry he wrote is out of vogue today, but vogues in poetry change almost as quickly and quite as surely as vogues in women's hats. He made us aware of the poetic possibilities in our own scenery and in our own customs; he wrote always in honesty and sincerity and with high purpose; he was himself a craftsman and he inspired others to be craftsmen; from first to last he encouraged the young poets around him, with no sense of envy or rivalry and with no thought of reward. I have not made extravagant claims for his literary merit, nor have I gone out of my way to emphasize his weaknesses. He did have many weaknesses; in particular, as if he felt that single-handedly he must create Canadian literature in all its branches, he tried to do too much, became a kind of literary jack-of-all-trades. But by virtue of his influence on others, and by virtue of the few truly excellent poems he himself wrote, he certainly deserves a place in our living tradition.

STANLEY R. MEALING ON

JOHN GRAVES SIMCOE

John Graves Simcoe was the first, and remains the best known, of the lieutenant-governors of this province. He was in Upper Canada for only four years (1792-6): a short time to build an enduring reputation, although not a particularly short term of office. Most of the governors of the British North American provinces before the late 1830's were relatively inconspicuous at the time and seem relatively unimportant now. As a group, they were of course an essential part of the machinery of colonial government. As individuals, they made little populair impact on the societies they governed and did little to shape their character or growth. They did not, as a rule, decisively influence the policy of the imperial government. They might, like Edmund Fanning, have a deep affection for their provinces. They might, like Sir Peregrine Maitland, raise a flutter in the narrow circle of official society. They might, like Lord Gosford, be armed with wonderfully good intentions. One of them was able to cap a minor career by an heroic death. But when they appear in the main stream of Canadian history it is generally because the growing demand for reform found them either formidable opponents or convenient targets. Their names are preserved, like flies in amber, in the history of Canadian self-government. In the main, their comings and goings constitute a formal parade to which Canadian historians are nearly as indifferent now as British North American farmers were then.

There are three clear exceptions: Lord Dorchester, Sir James

57

Craig, and Simcoe. Dorchester gave the better part of his working life to the government of Quebec—he was in North America for over thirty years—and was the author of an important constitution. Craig, at a critical point in the development of French-Canadian political consciousness, acted with mistaken decisiveness and gratuitously provided the cause of racial conflict with its first martyrs. Simcoe's career was different. He was not a constitution-maker. He did not interpret the society of the province to the government of the mother country. He did not turn discontent in the direction of rebellion. There were a number of schemes for which he was an enthusiast; only one of them was particularly his own idea, and none of them came to anything. He inaugurated a new constitution, but so did other governors; no hotels have been named after them. It is not immediately easy to see why his name should have survived better than that of Sir George Prevost, who certainly understood more thoroughly the policy he was expected to apply. Thomas Carleton had a shrewder estimate of the people he governed. Peter Hunter was a more business-like administrator. So was Sir John Colborne. Dalhousie, who served in British North America three times as long, was probably an altogether abler man. Yet Simcoe has received far more attention.

There have been in Canadian historiography two general attitudes towards Simcoe. One is deservedly dead, and I am doing what I can to mutilate the other. Five books and two biographical essays were published between 1900 and 1943. One of them is still seriously useful, if only because no document is more precious to the historian than a mistaken predecessor. The man these books describe stood high in the confidence of British ministers; in the House of Commons he was listened to, says D. C. Scott, with "more than ordinary attention"; in Upper Canada he was efficient, wise, beloved, and endowed with remarkable vision. His behaviour in the fall of 1794, when an American army was marching towards the border, is so fully described that one assumes it must have been important. His eulogies of the British constitution are cited with such emphasis that one assumes he really did transplant it, aristocracy and all, to Upper Canada. Sometimes I think these books were written about another man of the same name.

More recent and much better historians are not so impressed

by Simcoe the Maker of Canada. Professor Burt has indeed defended him against the attacks both of his main contemporary opponent, Lord Dorchester, and of his principal modern detractor, the American historian S. F. Bemis. Simcoe's support for the commercial ambitions of the St. Lawrence has also brought him rather more credit than he deserves. But his ideas, and particularly his strenuously vocal attachment to the British constitution, are now seen to have been commonplace in England and inappropriate to North America. He appears, not as the Burke of Upper Canada, but as an exponent of privilege on a frontier: just another Englishman who did not understand us. The point on which historians differ is how much he is to be excused for this, or how much he is to be blamed. The majority of unpublished opinion, I should think, inclines to blame him a good deal. Canadian history suffers from a lack of really colourful buffoons, and there is a standing temptation to cast Simcoe as a character comedian. There is even a danger of regarding him as on a par with such contemporaries of his as Colonel William Tatham, who subscribed to much the same political sentiments and who also traded in improbable minor projects. In 1796 he proposed a scheme for carrying goods up Niagara Falls "without any Boat, without the aid of Locks, and different from anything which has ever been exhibited" (Public Record Office, CO 42/320 and 107). What Tatham wanted from this plan was a land grant. What he got was a loan of £ 20 from the undersecretary of state. For a man who claimed descent from the royal houses of France and Spain, it was a modest settlement. A proposal to seize the Mississippi valley, made in 1793 by another such flimsy adventurer, Captain Charles Stevenson, has in fact been attributed to Simcoe. Although there are circumstances to excuse this mistake, it was a hundred and twenty-nine years before anybody made it.

Whether historians think that Simcoe's fervent platitudes indicate a foolish or merely a rigid mind, he remains for them as for his original biographers a creature of more than Tory orthodoxy and more than human enthusiasm. He is judged mainly by his ideas on colonial government. The result is to make him a figure representative of the imperial obstacles with which the emergence of autonomy and democracy in British North America had to contend. This is an accurate but an incomplete assessment. With perhaps two exceptions, historians have been interested in Simcoe as a symbolic rather than a real figure. I agree that his proper place in our history is as a symbol; but if we are going to pick the right symbol, we had better look at the man behind it.

A president of the American Historical Association has suggested that historians nowadays should resort to psychoanalysis for tasks like this. The examples of this historical *genre* that have appeared are not very encouraging; perhaps it is just as well that we know too little of Simcoe's private life to attempt it. His father was a naval officer who had risen by professional competence above the obscure parsons from whom he was descended. Simcoe's status as a gentleman of substance was based precariously on his father's and his own success until in 1784 he married an heiress. They had nine children. The effect of this marriage on his financial position is clear enough, but I have no idea what his family life was like. Perhaps a Freudian biographer would discover a father fixation in him. Certainly he was very proud of his father's record in the Seven Years' War, and naturally so. The war, which ended when Simcoe was eleven, had been unprecedentedly successful; it had been world-wide; and in Great Britain it had produced a wave of aggressive nationalism of a type which we are used to, but which was rare then. His father had been one of "Those Immortal Commanders" who in that war had "enlarged the Dominion and upheld the Majesty of these Kingdoms beyond the Idea of any former Age." Simcoe liked to believe that he had died playing a decisive role in the capture of Quebec. He wanted the ship that carried him to Canada to justify one of his father's ideas by sailing through the Gut of Canso. It was apparently from his father that he picked up the peculiar habit of referring diplomatic questions back to the Treaty of Utrecht, as well as the custom of pronouncing all fortifications indefensible. But his private character is a closed book, which I would not open if I could. I am interested only in his public behaviour.

He was a colonial governor for only six years, from the age of forty. For the greater part of his adult life (he died at fifty-four) he was a soldier, which was what he had been brought up to be. He was put under a military tutor at the age of fifteen, but by then it was probably unnecessary. When Simcoe was two years old his father had drawn up a set of maxims for the training of

his sons as officers (W. R. Riddell, *The Life of John Graves
Simcoe*, 32-5). They are excellent maxims: "Avoid quarrel-
ling ... "; "Let your obedience to the commands of Superior
Officers be exact, implicit and cheerful ... ," even if it should
"lead you instantly to sudden death . . . "; "Inure your body to
bear extremes of heat and cold, hunger and thirst, and exercise to
agility and strength by suitable toil"; "Exactitude is a necessary
quality, but affect not the martinet." Maxim number four, which
begins "Remember always that you are the servant of the
Public . . . ," ought perhaps to be in more general use.

Whether because of these maxims or not, Simcoe had a brilliant
career in the American Revolution. He rose from captain to lieu-
tenant-colonel in command of a Loyalist corps. At the expense of
three wounds, he acquired a reputation for dash. He was also a
conscientious, shrewd, and reliable commander, respected for and
very proud of his military science. He never lost a boyish enthusiasm for the details of his profession. Preparing to come to Upper
Canada, he was anxious to take along some brand-new weapons:
East India rockets and "the long three-pounders on carriages of
the new construction" (P.R.O., CO 42/316). The years he spent
fighting Americans were probably the happiest of his life. In
his years of unemployment on half-pay, 1783-1791, he concocted
a scheme for the capture of Cadiz and petitioned to be allowed to
raise a special mixed corps. It seems likely that in 1790 he would
have preferred service in a war against Spain to the administration of Upper Canada; but the Spanish would not fight. In the
border crisis of 1794 he professed himself eager to "do great
things with a small Army" (E. A. Cruikshank, *Correspondence of
John Graves Simcoe*, II, 354), and laid out an astonishing plan
of counterattack. Advancing in secret down the Ohio—a secrecy
to be combined with the distribution of manifestos—he was going
to capture Pittsburg, which the Americans would apparently not
defend. Then he would turn east and demonstrate that George
Washington was nothing but an amateur general.

After his colonial career he was given a territorial command in
the West Country. He at once bought a house by the sea, to be as
near as possible to a French invasion. When that did not come,
he cast his eye in several more exciting directions. He offered to
conquer central America. In 1799 he was mentioned to command

an expedition in support of the Chouans in Normandy and Brittany; but that was the year in which they collapsed. Then he was offered the post of second-in-command of a Mediterranean expedition, but he delayed his acceptance too long and the post eluded him. His dissatisfaction, on this occasion outspoken, increased when he failed in 1801 to become lieutenant-governor of Plymouth and in 1802 to become commander-in-chief in Ireland. He grew bitter about officers whose political connections were more fruitful than his, and especially resented "the Scotch officers with so unaccountable a preference for the English nation" (Ontario Archives, Simcoe Papers, letter of Dec. 3, 1805). At last persistence and a change in the ministry made him commander-in-chief in India. He was diverted to the joint command of an expedition to forestall Napoleon's invasion of Portugal. But he never got to fight the French. He fell ill and was carried back to die at Exeter on 26 October, 1806. His credentials to the court of Lisbon remained unopened in his papers until 1856.

But his interest, like his ambitions, ranged very far beyond soldiering. The essence of "Honor and Glory in the Service of my Country," was, as he saw it, the exercise of responsibility rather than the display of courage. The eleventh of his father's maxims refers hopefully, and as it turned out prophetically, to the French practice of choosing officers as governors of colonies. It was drilled into the young Simcoe that a properly trained officer was also a well-educated man.

The choice of good military authors is very small [runs maxim number fifteen], but for the honour of the military profession they are sufficient for all purposes and abound with the best precepts as examples, for civil and military life, and I hazard my reputation on this assertion that they are not only the best models for military conduct, but for conduct in every station of the patriot, courtier, statesman, magistrate, and finished gentleman.

(Riddell, 3-5)

Simcoe had at least the pretensions of a finished gentleman. He was able to complain that society in Montreal and Quebec, where he spent the winter of 1791-2, contained "few men of learning and information" (J. R. Robertson, *The Diary of Mrs. John Graves Simcoe,* 81). He was proud of his close reading of Tacitus, Xenophon, and military history, particularly the history of the

English Civil Wars and of the German campaigns in the Seven Year's War. He seems to have been confident of his general knowledge of English history. He was complimented on his "great love and Cognizance of Science in every branch" (P.R.O., CO 42/317), and if the compliment is suspect as coming from a petitioner, the petitioner was the son of a friend who may have designed it to flatter a particular vanity. The eighteenth-century enlightenment, however, passed him by. He had no use for egg-heads, even when they kept out of politics. One of his favourite objects of denunciation was "the Minute, the Plebian, the Mechanical Philosophy which ... from the successful and problematical experiments of its Professors in natural enquiries, has assumed to itself the claim of dictating in religion and Morality" (Cruikshank, III, 351). At times he did not distinguish between "Philosophists and Frenchmen." He refused to be guided by "the suspicious data of the insidious Occonomist" (Riddell, 279). He was, however, not guilty of what military governors are commonly accused of, the neglect of economic matters. His dislike of merchants was active—the statements of merchants, he warned, were to be regarded with caution—but unlike the earlier governors of Quebec or his contemporary in Prince Edward Island he came into no conflict with those under his government. He was as full of projects for the commercial development of Upper Canada as for its anglicization. In Saint Domingo, where he was also governor for a time, he was careful to pay attention to the island's American commerce—far more than was paid to it by the civilian French Jacobin commissioners. He was even capable of so unsoldierly a practice as using a commercial metaphor when writing about religion to a bishop.

Simcoe had an immense stock of minor projects about which he did not have the prudence to remain silent. He said that since Upper Canada's was a new government he could adopt "a more diffusive mode of correspondence than would otherwise be necessary or suitable" (Cruikshank, III, 141); and this was a threat which he carried out to the full. He proposed to have hats manufactured in the province, although it no longer had any important share in the fur trade. He wanted to found a university without waiting for schools. He endorsed a scheme to print instalments from the *Encyclopaedia Britannica*, which was not yet published, in newspapers which did not exist. He was sure that there were valuable iron mines to be developed, and a commercial sturgeon fishery. He suggested that Upper Canada might replace the Carolinas as a source of indigo. He wanted to enlist the sons of principal inhabitants as ensigns in the 60th Regiment, giving them the military education that had done so much for himself. The regiment was in the West Indies at the time, and would have had to be brought away. The great majority of his ideas were innocent of any development once he had got them. They went around and around in his head, and they appear and reappear in his dispatches. Nor was he content to hold commonplace ideas in their ordinary isolation from one another. The contents of his brain appear to have been so closely interconnected that almost anything he wrote implies almost everything else. By incessant activity his various schemes and opinions had arranged themselves into an order, not in itself logical or necessary—they formed something more like a drill manual than a philosophy—but very definite. In his own words, he "proceeded upon a system." He did not think; he bubbled. He was our only effervescent governor.

It is time to enter a caveat. There is a biblical injunction: "Blessed is the man that ... sitteth not in the seat of the scornful." The eighteenth century is a long way from us, and its nuances are not easy to recapture. None of these schemes, laboriously set in its proper context, is as wild as it sounds. They were for the most part the offhand products of a natural ignorance, nearly all conceived before Simcoe had sailed for the province. It is true that only a strangely innocent and brash man would have addressed them to a secretary of state. They are not much less defensible than the creation of a university at Peterborough, or the continued existence of the Canadian Senate, or the Canadian Bill of Rights in its present form. Simcoe had a substratum of common sense, which, if it did not check his pen, did govern his actions. Of all his minor projects, he actually tried to implement only one. He nearly poisoned his troops by feeding them locally cured pork. He did not know that curing pork for use the next winter was quite different from curing it for use a full year later. Not many people did.

Ever since the end of the American war, Upper Canada had been the focus of Simcoe's continued interest in North America.

64

He knew a group of Loyalists in London who had a sharp eye on the lands of the province. With his appointment as lieutenant-governor his interest became, for a while, a passion. While the fit was on him he offered to combine his post with that of ambassador to the United States. He suggested that his usefulness in negotiations over the boundary would be enhanced if he were allowed to defeat the American secretary of state in a public debate. He repeated the worn-out beliefs of ten years before that the Americans did not really want independence, that they could never unite, and that if they did Vermont and Kentucky would never join them. His headiest proposals for converting Americans all depended on the position or the example of Upper Canada, "the Spot destined by Nature to govern the interior world" (Cruikshank, I, 18).

One of Simcoe's grand schemes for the North American continent was for trade in the interior by way of the St. Lawrence. There was nothing original about it, and not even very much that was peculiar. It came in two instalments, one when he was appointed to Upper Canada and one after he had been there for a couple of years. In the first, the western posts were important, especially Detroit, and there were political overtones of varying intensity, directed at Vermont or Kentucky. In the second, the route to the interior had shifted west of Lake Michigan, and the western posts did not matter. The change came before Jay's Treaty, although not before Simcoe had seen Detroit and pronounced it indefensible. Most of his arguments for both versions were severely mercantilist. This involved him in the contention that Upper Canada, 250 miles upstream from the nearest port and separated from it by rapids over which the water was less than a foot deep, was in effect on the seacoast. But better men than he found difficulty in extending the mercantilist justification of empire to the province, and his invocation of it was purely conventional. The first version was a very flimsy affair. It was really little more than an argument for retaining the western posts (then, at least as he believed, the intention of the British government) with some odd pieces of information showing how complete an American expert Simcoe was. One of the oddest of these, which came from his father, was that "with the assistance of a few sluices" Montreal might preside over a continuous waterway from

Hudson's Bay to the Gulf of Mexico (Cruikshank, I, 8). In one way it was an excellent scheme; nobody could object to it except for its being impracticable, and its details were too vague to make such a charge serious. It was a defence of the commercial value of interior settlements by a man just appointed to govern one.

The second version was very difficult. It was well-informed, well worked out, and I think may be called realistic except in its expectation of government expenditure and its prediction of British policy. These were of course fatal weaknesses, because it was submitted just when the British government was deciding, in Jay's Treaty, to reach the interior markets of the continent by free rather than mercantilist trade. For an appreciation of Simcoe, the significant thing about this second scheme is that it was not his. One part of it, a plan for a fur-trading factory west of Lake Michigan, was based on the obvious analogy of current American practice and more precisely on the memorial of a Detroit fur trader. The other part, a plan for the manufacture and export of flour, was suggested by a Niagara merchant. What Simcoe did was to remove any suggestion of local monopolies and to elaborate the claims of advantage to the mother country as well as to the colony. Apart from that, nothing was his but the adjectives, although of course he presented the whole thing as the product of his advanced ideas. I am not bringing a charge of plagiarism; it was no part of his duty to supply foot-notes to his dispatches, and the two inspiring memoranda were sent to the Committee for Trade along with a dozen other enclosures (P.A.C., q 280-2 and Cruikshank, III, 52-70). The point to be insisted on is that in this scheme Simcoe was entirely in sympathy with the aspirations of Upper Canada and entirely out of touch with Westminster. The facts to which he was most blind were not those of North America. In so far as he tried to support the plan by dwelling on its special advantages to the mother country, he was turning British arguments to Canadian purposes.

Commercial advantages had to be a part of any imperial design, and Simcoe's real design was to make Upper Canada a thriving and important colony. It was to this that his nebulous enthusiasm for the American world was finally reduced. The plan to encourage the manufacture of flour put most of its emphasis on the prosperity of the province, an emphasis not inconsistent with, but tending to overshadow, its usefulness to the Empire. It was only natural that the internal prosperity of Upper Canada should be the more immediate object of his attention, since it was more purely his responsibility. Naturally, also, it was for the province's own benefit that he recommended its Assembly to enact whatever might give "clear and evident Security to the Possessor of Capitals in the British Empire" who might be willing to invest in land (P.R.O., CO 42/319). No consideration of circumstances, however, or of the limits to his share in regulating the imperial economy, can explain away the fact that Simcoe's aim was political. Upper Canada had to be prosperous to convince its inhabitants of the merit of the imperial connection. They would, he wrote, be "attached to the British Government or hostile to it by the result of their own comparison and investigation." Even "those who may not see the necessity and immense advantage of experience in the form of Government ... may be attached to it by the undisturbed possession of present benefits and the prospect of future advantages for their families" (Cruikshank, III, 67-8). Simcoe intended to prove not so much that his colonists were good for the Empire as that the Empire was good for them.

It was a merit of Simcoe's, for which he is not often given credit, that he had a very ready sympathy for the aspirations of the people he governed. He was to show it later in Saint Domingo, where the British intervened in a complicated racial war. In Upper Canada it led him to set about the land-granting problem with special zeal, which if it did not settle much was at least well meant. He is said never to have refused anyone an audience, and he certainly forwarded with approval some memorials that his superiors made short work of. "He has," wrote Chief Justice Osgoode, "a benevolent heart without much discrimination" (J. E. Middleton and F. Landon, *The Province of Ontario*, I, 76). His manner was "simple, plain and obliging" (La Rochefoucauld-Liancourt, *Travels*, I, 430). His receptiveness probably bordered on credulity, but it was no bad qualification for his post, where easy personal relations were of real importance. His subordinate officials were a mixed lot, dissatisfied with their positions. While he was in the province, they worked harmoniously, if not well; it was only some years after his departure that the clerk of the Executive Council shot the attorney-general. Simcoe's dispatches did bristle with animosities, but towards people at a distance, and generally towards his superiors. His only important critic in Upper Canada, the Kingston merchant Richard Cartwright, stopped his criticisms after they had met. Earlier, the two had written bitter nonsense about one another. Apparently the charm at which his wife's diary hints was real; but mere amiability was not the main part of the story. The fact is that Simcoe, who spent all his life in government service or in seeking after it and who was forever extolling subordination, never acquired the official outlook. He had no skill at all in gauging or predicting ministerial emphasis. The whole of his correspondence, from all his posts, has the character of a debate between metropolitan official and local enthusiast.

But by the beginning of 1794 his most frequently expressed ground for insisting on the importance of Upper Canada was military. He thought that the lower province was a hotbed of sedition, and kept a wary eye on the French Canadians within his own jurisdiction; the American Congress was scarcely more dangerous. The defence of which Upper Canada proved itself capable in the war of 1812 cannot be said altogether to have confirmed his judgment, for he went so far as to maintain that the upper province could be held if the lower were lost, whereas the reverse was not true. When it seemed that Wayne might attack Detroit, he predicted the loss of both Canadas if the post fell. After his return to England, he sent the Duke of Portland his considered ideas on the defence of the Canadas. Invasion by a French fleet, he thought, was not very difficult, and if the main body of British troops were kept at Quebec they would in such an event be by-passed while the habitants were led in revolt. As strong a force at Montreal as at Quebec was necessary, but even it would be inadequate against an American invasion, coupled as it was bound to be with "an universal insurrection of the French Canadians." To meet that danger required a force in Upper Canada as large as the other two combined. With this force, "to which the Indians might coalesce and a Loyal Militia rally," his province would answer for the safety of the rest (E. A. Cruikshank and A. F. Hunter, *Correspondence of the Honourable Peter Russell*, I, 104–5). Simcoe had meant what he wrote three years earlier; he thought Upper Canada was "the Bulwark of the British Empire in America" (Cruikshank, II, 104).

It is not surprising that Simcoe's preference for Upper Canada should finally have taken a predominantly military form. From about the middle of 1793, the bulk of his correspondence is concerned with Indians and Americans, with danger and the ways to meet it. He had told Dundas to begin with that the leading feature of all his plans was "the wise Principle (at least such it appears to me) of blending civil and military Advantages" (Cruikshank, I, 82). His constant refrain was that in every establishment military and civil concerns were too "intimately blended" to be separated. In Saint Domingo this conviction gave impetus to his reform of the civil administration. In this country it led to his long squabble with Dorchester and to the experiment of the Queen's Rangers.

Simcoe thought of himself as coming out more to found than to govern Upper Canada, and, to an even greater extent than he is accused of, he meant to do so by working from recognized models. Those models were the British constitution and the Roman military colony. To admire the first was ordinary, but to have considered the second at all was originality of a kind. He knew that the first land grants had been largely to disbanded soldiers, and, forgetting that the leadership of ex-officers had been rejected, he supposed that the Loyalist settlements retained a military character. Further, he wanted to provide more surely military nuclei for new settlement in the winter quarters of his provincial corps, the Queen's Rangers, "Stations to be judiciously selected for the Quarters of the King's Troops," he was still explaining at the end of 1795, "is in my System and Opinion, the only basis on which Towns will speedily and inevitably arise" (Cruikshank, IV, 156). The alternative was settlement "incoherent in every particular, not to be relied on by Government" (Cruikshank, IV, 339-40). In his original presentation of the scheme he had made the Roman analogy explicit. A chain of military *coloniae* in the Ontario peninsula was to act as it had for the Romans on the Rhine; it was to ensure the security and allegiance and to mould the character of a frontier.

Simcoe's definite reference to the Roman practice was unusual. He may have got it from Tacitus. He may also have got it from a book written by his first commanding officer. In itself, however, the ideal of social cohesion was commonplace. The use of troops to attain it, while distinct from their incidental use to promote settlement, was so like the latter as to pass for the same thing. Simcoe himself never made the distinction entirely clear, and ministers certainly ignored it. Dundas seems to have been most struck by the prospect of economy. He recommended the Queen's Rangers to the House of Commons as a means of avoiding the full expense of sending regular troops. Economy had not been so evident in Simcoe's original proposal for twelve companies, including cavalry and military artificers. The artificers were almost a "system" in themselves, but in spite of Pitt's momentary favour they joined the list of Simcoe's "Public disappointments." Even as actually established, with two infantry companies, the Rangers cost nearly £ 400 a year more than had been anticipated. In informing Dorchester of the corps' existence, Dundas was enthusiastic, but he emphasized its normal military function. This dispatch and his speech in Parliament were hardly what Simcoe claimed, "stipulations" that he was free to devote the Rangers entirely to the establishment of his *coloniae*. In fact the only just statement of his programme for the corps ever made except by himself was that of Fox in objecting to its establishment, and Fox may have meant to draw a caricature.

In practice, the Queen's Rangers turned out to be a quite normal body of men. It is difficult to find in anything they actually did the fruits of Tacitus' inspiration or of a specially intimate blend of civil and military objects. Some people may take this as a defence of Simcoe's common sense; he took it as a grievance. The temptation to use the corps as ordinary troops was strong when there was a war on, and when ministers had always regarded it as a sort of labour battalion anyway. Ministers would make no exception to the rule that Dorchester was commander-in-chief, and Dorchester would make no exception to the rule that garrison and communications duties were the main purpose of troops. On 9 June, 1796, he forbade the establishment of any new posts in the upper province, and that put an end to Simcoe's peninsular *coloniae*. The corps was by then so thinly officered that its discipline was poor, and the men were likely to desert if given too much work. Confirmed in the role of normal troops, not social prophets, and not even relied on to build roads, the Queen's Rangers were disbanded in the general reduction of 1802.

In the beginning at least, the *coloniae* were part of a larger plan. Around them new settlers were to "coalesce into the general principles of British subjects" (Cruikshank, IV, 54). What Simcoe proposed for Upper Canada in the first instance was meticulous, instantaneous, and uncompromising assimilation to British models. The process was not to be confined to the political framework or to the fostering of a local aristocracy. There would be, he wrote before his appointment was formal, "causes ... perpetually offering themselves" for the practice of assimilation (Cruikshank, V, 247). "Customs, Manners and Principles" (Cruikshank, I, 27) were all supposed to follow the flag. This was of course far beyond the intention behind the Constitutional Act. Its aim was to strengthen the colonial executives by giving them social support. In the thirteen colonies, and in Ireland, executives had come to grief because they had been unsupported from below; when the Act was being passed there were lesser but similar troubles in Barbados and Dominica. The Legislative Council, the titles of honour, and in part the Clergy Reserves were an attempt to supply the deficiency, without departing from representative government. Beyond this attempt, which was very short-lived, there was only the vague assumption of a general similarity that had underlain English colonization since the days when it went no farther afield than Ireland, and that was by no means peculiar to British colonies. Simcoe far exceeded his superiors in presenting assimilation as an object *per se*; but he did so only in words, and he was consistent in doing that only in the first flush of enthusiasm. It is a little unfair to pin him too closely to his later oratory. If his speeches to the Assembly are to be taken literally, they probably indicate more zeal for the French war than for the British constitution.

The first three sessions of the provincial legislature did pass several measures that can be represented as instances of meticulous assimilation, but they really belong to the older and vaguer tradition. They can be matched from the statutes of New England or Jamaica, and I think they would have been much the same if the Constitutional Act had never left Grenville's closet or Simcoe had died of one of his wounds in the American war. Generally, the test of action reduces his anglicization fever to a temperature little above normal. His conduct of administration was decidedly autocratic, quite as much so in Upper Canada as later in Saint Domingo, where there was no question of following British models and where his powers as governor were very wide. The proposal for municipal corporations, which the Duke of Portland vetoed, was hardly a piece of meticulous assimilation. In any case, it was Richard Cartwright's scheme, not Simcoe's. Simcoe justified his lieutenants of counties on practical as well as Messianic grounds, by the need in so large a colony for "a gradation of Officers" (Cruikshank, IV, 116). In the perfect autocracy of Saint Domingo he made rather similar appointments. In administration his fetish was efficiency—"neither a *sine cure* mind nor a *sine cure* body throughout the whole Province" (Cruikshank, I, 34). He was so full of that ideal that there was little room for any other.

Nor did he really rely on the excellence of transplanted British institutions to attract and convert Americans. "The preference for the British form of Government is alledged by some for quitting the States," he wrote, "but the Oppression of the Land Jobbers and the uncertainty of the Titles is the more general reason" (Cruikshank, II, 109-10). The simple fact was that Upper Canada needed settlers if it was to grow and that there was only one place to get them. He would have preferred, until Dundas objected, to transplant the population of Newfoundland; but he had a high opinion of New Englanders as colonists. When he invited "those who shall prefer the British Constitution in Upper Canada" (Cruikshank, I, 152), it meant no more than those who were not openly determined to bring the American constitution with them. To the end of his residence in the colony he could still write of defeating "the spirit of democratic subversion in the very Country which gave it existence and growth" (Cruikshank, III, 265), but in practice he gave more weight to Upper Canada's economic growth than to its constitutional purity. In his later memorials he did not claim to have given the province a British character, but only to have preserved its British connection.

Assimilation existed on three levels: as an old and flexible assumption that colonies were transplanted societies with their institutions at least rooted in the mother country; in the Constitutional Act, as a political device for strengthening the executive; and in some of Simcoe's utterances, as an end in itself. There is no certain way of deciding how much of his early effusions he seriously intended to implement. His actions never approached the first and did not even amount to the second. Of course the kind of assimilation he advocated in his most exalted moments was too wildly impracticable to be more than preached; to demand its application is rather like questioning the sincerity of a revivalist who cannot produce God in the flesh. Nor is the reality of his intention to transplant the British constitution "in every Branch and Advantage" disproved by a certain tendency to confuse it with the British army. Simcoe was quite capable of bridging the gap between his personal autocracy and a hypothetical aristocracy by the assumption, to which he was prone, that everybody agreed with him. There is no certain way of deciding how much he seriously intended to implement and how much he simply found it satisfying or thought it acceptable to say. His hopes of transplanting everything in England except the people were never so well articulated as to constitute a plan and never so central to his intentions as to constitute a mission. They were less the crude convictions of a platitudinous mind than the conventional utterances of an ambitious man. Simcoe was not primarily a secular Messiah, he was a careerist. His zeal cannot be separated from his ambition. I should no more suggest that the one was assumed than that the other was discreditable; but his enthusiasm for his various projects is not to be compared with his enthusiasm for himself.

Moreover, his ambition was deliberate and calculating. In the American war he had chosen the command of a light corps because it was "generally esteemed the best mode of instruction for those who aim at higher stations" (Simcoe, *Military Journal*, 13-14). As soon as he got his appointment to Upper Canada he forgot how much he had solicited it, made a virtue of acceptance and began to look forward to a reward "in future trusts, and more lucrative employments" (P.R.O., CO 42/316). He was an assiduous although unskilful memorialist. It was not the least function of his dispatches to advertise his devotion to duty. The peculiar mixture of fire and platitudes that is their hallmark owed much to his inept determination to follow up any hint ministers gave him. As he put it himself, "nothing is more essential than to profess Correct Opinions, unless to possess a *correct* Acquaintance" (Ontario Archives, Simcoe Papers, letter of Oct. 23, 1801). Since his ambition outran his talents, he deliberately sought after original, ingenious, and "enlarged" designs. After the event, he was always prepared for any emergency. In his search for triumphs he came at last to appropriate other people's mistakes; he claimed that the reoccupation of Fort Miamis in 1794 had been his idea and that it had been the master-stroke averting war. He had no knack for the choice of patrons—he backed Clinton against Cornwallis and Addington against Pitt—so that he suffered many disappointments. Once he was back in regular military employment he lost his interest in British North America. He did once express a desire to return; that was when he thought the Duke of Portland had promised to make him governor-in-chief, and even then he wanted a peerage as well. His ambition was too volatile not to be heated by any situation he might be in. The minor plans and major enthusiasms for which he can be ridiculed should, I think, be regarded chiefly as frenetic attemps to call attention to himself. If he is to be judged by his actions in Upper Canada, he was in the main competent and sensible. By this standard he was also comparatively unimportant.

So far, I have been defending Simcoe's sanity at the expense of his reputation. His importance, however, depends far more on his words than on whatever he meant to do about them. In the twenty years after he left Upper Canada it continued to be settled by American immigrants. Upper Canada was as much the product of American expansion as Kentucky or Vermont, and its society was much the same. The war of 1812, however, revived the loyalist tradition and attached it to the local oligarchy which by that time really governed the province. That oligarchy perpetuated Simcoe's habit of saying, what was obviously false, that Upper Canada had not merely a British government but the British constitution. Reformers were therefore pushed into the position of criticizing not only their own government but that of the mother country as well. They found that, as it applied to them, the constitution was "like the north-eastern boundary of the United States; it is neither here, nor there, and yet is presumed to be everywhere." The result was statements like this:

74

Correctly speaking, there is no such thing in existence. There is, doubtless, plenty of governing power in England; but, as to a Constitution, or supreme law regulative of that power, there is no such thing. The British government is made up of old usages, old charters, old fictions, and old prejudices ... the whole, together, presenting a standing, and wonderfully lasting, scheme of mystification.

(D. M'Leod, *Settlement of Upper Canada, 14-15*)

This cannot be called incorrect, but it was called seditious. It was not a position likely to make reform practical politics. In the end, reformers avoided it only through Robert Baldwin's feat of constitutional analysis. The Family Compact found in Simcoe's utterances a convenient myth to justify its own claims, as well as a convenient statement of its own beliefs.

Simcoe did more than set a pattern of distorting the Loyalist tradition in the direction of social conservatism and political reaction. From the moment that he entered Upper Canada, he became its defender against the lower province. When he was not allowed to annex Montreal, he prevented Montreal speculators from getting Upper Canadian lands. I have recounted his insistence on the greater strategic importance of the upper province, on its greater loyalty and its brighter commercial future. These may have been less important to him than a personal and administrative quarrel with the governor at Quebec. As commander-in-chief, Lord Dorchester was his superior all the time; as governor-in-chief, Dorchester had authority over Upper Canada only if he came into it. The two most enduring of Simcoe's enthusiasms were for the Queen's Rangers and, in a general way, for the province itself. Both became focussed on his attempt to escape from Dorchester's control as commander-in-chief. He did not succeed, except for getting the Indian Department away from military control. In the attempt, however, he made the direct defence of Upper Canadian interests a part of his "system." It remained a central part of the Tory credo under the Family Compact. It survived the Compact's disintegration. Emphasis on it was not entirely displaced from the programme of the Liberal-Conservative coalition until the retirement of John Hillyard Cameron in 1857. By that time sectionalism was the special preserve of the Grits, whose radicalism left conservatives to look after local interests by bargaining with the lower province, not by trying to break the union of 1841. The first important Conservative I know of who crossed over to the Liberal camp for sectional reasons was R. W. Scott in 1871. He joined Blake's provincial cabinet, explaining rather shamefacedly to Sir John Macdonald that he had to look after the lumber trade, the Central Canada Railway, and the municipal debt of the city of Ottawa.

Simcoe gave timely and concise expression to both the political creed and the economic basis of Upper Canadian Toryism. He was not original, except in a trivial way; he was only intense. But he was also sensitive to his environment. By combining sectionalism with it, he helped to adapt Toryism to a new society and gave it a genuine function in politics. He was not its founder, but he was its first and its most complete spokesman. So far as it was possible or necessary for one man to do so, he crystallized it. There is no wonder that it should for a long time have canonized him.

SAINT-DENYS-GARNEAU

The birth of a work is like the birth of a child. There is a kind of splendour in the birth of a child, and yet, seen at close range, it is not always beautiful—at least not to those who see life in terms of pretty pictures. We must face the fact that life often lacks distinction, and perhaps nowhere more conspicuously than in the act of birth, at the very moment when it reaches the height of its powers. Man, moreover, who is the supreme manifestation of life on earth, does not carry on the work of civilization with the good manners which Dale Carnegie teaches to those who would become his friends.

The age of crinoline and lace, with its military glories, its diplomatic intrigues, its flowery rhetoric, has passed away. Man no longer wishes to stop at externals; behind the play of ideas he wishes to discover the yearnings of the soul. He no longer asks of life that it amuse him, as if he were capable of forgetting his misery and his greatness. He asks that it satisfy his needs—above all, that it enable him to fulfil himself.

To tell the story of the work of Saint-Denys-Garneau is to tell the story of a birth about which we know little more than the fears with which it began and the convulsions with which it ended. The circumstances would appear to have been so unfavourable that we might well expect the worst. But the work has survived its author. Indeed it has grown in stature since his death, and it has encouraged less difficult births.

I should like to stress here that the fulfilment of the destiny of

77

this poet is closely bound up with the fulfilment of the destiny of the French-Canadian people, who have wished very much to escape from an isolation which threatens to suffocate them, yet to do so without sacrificing their identity. Neither case held much promise of success; but it seems to me that about fifty poems and the *Journal* of Saint-Denys-Garneau proclaim a liberation which other works by other writers have since confirmed.

Saint-Denys-Garneau was born in Montreal in 1912, but he was to spend all his summers and even several whole years at the Manoir de Ste. Catherine de Fossambault near Quebec, which he had inherited from his maternal great-grandfather, the *seigneur* of Beauport. On his father's side he was the grandson of the poet Alfred Garneau, and the great-grandson of the historian François-Xavier Garneau. Like most children of the French-Canadian *bourgeoisie*, he attended the "classical" college; but his decision to become a writer led him to turn aside from a university education. He wrote the slender yet important body of work upon which his reputation rests in the four years between 1935 and 1939. His *Journal* stops at the beginning of 1939, and his correspondence extends only a little beyond 1941. He was to die tragically on October 24, 1943, at the age of 31.

It is 1935, then, and we go to meet a young man of twenty-three at the moment when he is experiencing the crucial revelation of his vocation as a poet. It is a time when he feels that his life is threatened, and he is forced to recognize that death is one of the faces of life. Fresh from college and its frustrating round of intellectual gymnastics, he enters a society whose leaders lack the imagination necessary to break loose from the machinery of a bankrupt economy. Thousands of men rotting in idleness are receiving only a meagre pittance, while others find nothing better to do than to set fire to mountains of wheat and dump tons of coffee into the sea. The war has not yet imposed its drastic remedies. Men of good-will protest; but they can do little more than cry out that a human being is worth more than the machines he runs, and that his life should be saved at any cost and become the principal concern of those who bring down the budgets. It is a time of misery, but is is also a time of fervour. People search passionately for a way out; they remember Marx, but they remember also the Sermon on the Mount.

Saint-Denys-Garneau did not have to wonder where the next meal was coming from, but he could not remain insensible to the cry of the distressed, to the universal hunger for justice. He could perhaps have let everything go and life would have been easy for him if he had not had to answer questions whose gravity astonished him, and if he had not felt constantly the need to pass beyond appearances in order to make contact with reality—with his fellow-men, and, more profoundly, with that immutable presence which would represent his true self.

We meet Saint-Denys-Garneau again in Montreal—a city which is in a constant state of turmoil from expansion whose end cannot yet be foreseen, a noisy and disordered city. He lived in a sheltered *milieu,* and with his friends he turned his attention to all those things whose existence he had, as a student, only suspected: long sessions of music, visits to art exhibits, interminable discussions, and other, shall we say, less intellectual diversions. This life continued in the country during the summer months, at Ste. Catherine, where an exuberant nature offered a spectacle more beautiful than that of the great city, but in many ways no less confused. This countryside, like many others, has not been humanized, and it leaves us often with an impression of brutality. It will not be conquered until some memorial of great beauty which affirms the presence of man lightens and deepens its poetry. This scenery is not reassuring: the houses seem often temporary shelters, and in the limpid atmosphere the very dark greens and the very cold blues clash.

On the grey streets of Montreal or on the dusty roads in the hills of Portneuf one could meet this young man who gave evidence of so much talent, but in whom one sensed also much that was unpredictable and disquieting. In his bursts of laughter, as in his sadness, there was something excessive; yet one could believe that he was enough of a conformist to bow at least to literary conventions, if not to those of the world.

In this summer of 1935, however, Saint-Denys-Garneau already knew that he was not one of those people who invariably succeed in doing what they wish to do; it would not be easy for him to follow the lead of his treacherous nature. Here begins the adventure, for it was in the course of this summer that he wrote the first poems which bear the mark of his personality. They are poems in which the principal themes of his work are already taking form.

At the moment at which he invites us to come with him into his world, he examines himself, with a gravity mixed with disquiet, on the powers of language to which he is abandoning himself. This is the dawn, but we shall emerge very soon into the full light of mid-day. He sums up this first stage of his self-exploration in "Habitation du paysage," whose opening words evoke joy:

Au souffle frais du matin, c'est un peintre qui part en rêve et part en chasse, le pas allègre ... c'est un peintre qui promène ce qu'il est parmi ce qu'il y a.

But suddenly the landscape is turned upside down, and, without the painter-poet having moved, there he is at the other side of the world:

On voit que quelque chose se fait plus clair pour lui et plus mystérieux; qu'il est en train de recomposer une figure déjà amorcée en quelque part de lui-même; mais il a peur, il hésite encore à dire: c'est ma sœur!

Who is she, and how will he catch up with her? Only through words. If he puts to work the disturbing powers of poetry, perhaps he will discover the language that will make her arise from the shadows and at the same time lift him up to her:

Il hésite devant cette confrontation définitive qui consiste à mettre un nom sur ce qui n'en a pas encore. Est-il assez beau le nom que nous avons? Va-t-il nous rapprocher de celle que nous aimons, ou nous la voiler à jamais?

His life is committed to this search for the magic word. If he should lose his way and never discover the one word which is fitting, he will never be able to make contact with this mysterious reality without which life is not worth living. In the beautiful prose-poem which he called "Monologue sur le mot," Saint-Denys-Garneau speaks at length of this passionate dependence on the creative word.

Je me suis éveillé en face du monde des mots. J'ai entendu l'appel des mots. J'ai senti la terrible exigence des mots qui ont soif de substance. Hélas! tant de dialogues meurent avant la fin et une voix continue à psalmodier dans l'absence qui s'épaissit.

80

Once more the poet is alone and more vulnerable than ever. "Il est libre du mot parce qu'il le possède, parce que le mot est lui-même en quelque sorte." But this word "n'est pas à lui seul une connaissance, mais le signe d'une connaissance. D'où sa terrible exigence." The poet is not in himself a god, but the image of God; whence the fearful demands of his vocation.

The poet does not deform the word, but he dominates its form in a unique way.

[Il] possède sa forme d'unique façon. Et quand il dit *oiseau* il peut n'avoir aucun souvenir d'oiseau, aucun autre modèle que cette part en lui de lui-même qui est oiseau et qui répond à l'appel de son nom par un vol magnifique en plein air et le déploiement vaste de ses ailes.

And when the poet comes to pronounce other marvellous words such as "night" and "love", what heights will he not be lifted to then? Always he pronounces these words for the first time, and the communication which he establishes disturbs us as if no one else had ever known these realities. The word (*mot*) must raise itself to the dignity of a language (*parole*) which destroys the solitude of all things.

Until the very end Saint-Denys-Garneau questioned himself about the powers of poetry, about the word become language; and it is in the posthumous poems especially (*Poésies Complètes,* 1949) that he explains himself most completely. In "Silence," and in the four poems which follow "Silence," he tells us that "toutes paroles lui deviennent intérieures." All that we call language, all that is born of the coupling of two words in an intimate embrace, has become for him an intensely inward experience. And occasionally, thanks to this act of love, there is accomplished in the soul the meeting of the temporal and the eternal, "l'ineffable identité où prend lumière tout le poème." Elsewhere he tells us that this victory is uncertain and even a kind of mockery:

> Identité
> Toujours rompue
> Le nœud s'est mis à sentir
> Les tours de corde dont il est fait.

What happens during these four years of literary production that should concern us especially? Outwardly, very little. Already two years have passed since Saint-Denys-Garneau abandoned his studies, and he is painting and writing, but very little. He contributes regularly, however, to a little magazine, *La Relève,* which some of his friends have started. But his work does not really begin until the commencement of his journal in January, 1935, in which, from the outset, he speaks to us of an "expérience intérieure délaissement, d'humiliation, de solitude," a crisis at once psychological and spiritual which is to grow more acute and which is to govern the development of his poetry. Yet each poem is to be a moment of transcendency carrying us to the very limits of human powers.

For Saint-Denys-Garneau, two events normal to the life of the spirit but usually separated by years happen simultaneously. At the age of twenty-three he has a decisive encounter with his destiny, which is the discovery of his vocation as a poet, and another encounter with death, which reveals to him at the same time the true face of life. Such revelations are not accomplished without crises, and even the most vigorous of spirits has been unable to overcome the initial shock they bring.

In a passage in his *Confessions,* Tolstoi describes this experience of death, which he was not to have until he was forty-seven, in terms very similar to those which Saint-Denys-Garneau uses in his *Journal.* "Five years ago," Tolstoi relates, "something strange began to stir in me. First there were moments of astonishment, of arrested life, as if I did not know how to live or how to act; and I became distressed and sad. . . . What happened to me happens to anyone who falls ill of an incurable disease. First the minute symptoms of the disease appear, which the victim ignores; then these symptoms occur with increasing regularity and finally become a specific and sustained pain. The pain increases and the sick man is suddenly confronted with the fact that this thing, which he has taken to be a mere indisposition, is that one thing more important to him than anything else in the world: Death." Tolstoi adds, "I felt that the ground on which I stood was falling away, that there was no longer anything that I could hold on to, that what I lived by was gone, and that I had nothing to put in its place."

During his lifetime, Saint-Denys-Garneau published only a slender collection of poems called *Regards et jeux dans l'espace,* and some twenty articles in *La Relève,* the modest periodical whose young collaborators expressed awkwardly some of the hidden aspirations of their *milieu*. They were convinced that to withdraw into oneself, to consent to isolation, no matter how comfortable it might be, was for a community as for an individual to renounce life. On the contrary, they thought the proper solution was to immerse themselves in the excitement of the present, to participate in the quest undertaken by those who were proposing new remedies for new problems. They felt compelled to do this even at the risk of seeing a mere anxiety change into an anguish which neither communism, nor assuredly fascism, nor the timid responses of a capitalism rotten with unemployment could allay.

The young French Canadian of 1930—and were things really any different for the young English Canadian?—however much he might want to travel, was forced to recognize that he was stranded, and that the view of life that was offered to him in his isolation was anything but universal. He had first to break through the barrier which compelled him to live in the past—that is to say, in an unreal world. Though the voices of great men reached him from the other side of the wall, he himself had to shout to make himself heard. This is not the way civilized men carry on a conversation. But what else can one do if one is to gain freedom?

When *Regards et jeux dans l'espace* appeared in 1937 the professional critics did not understand the importance of these thirty poems; but there were some young people who at least suspected that the twenty-five-year-old poet was trying to say something important to them. This was all the more surprising since the sources of this poetry and the inward experience of which it was born were not to be revealed clearly until much later, with the appearance in 1949 of some poems which the author, significantly enough, had not dared to publish earlier, and with the appearance in 1954 of the *Journal*.

Unquestionably, *Regards et jeux dans l'espace* is an invaluable revelation of a spiritual drama, of the cries of pain which are calls for liberty and joy, and which already, thanks to the mysterious powers of poetry, evoke forcefully the opposite of what they decry: love transcending hate, peace transcending fear. Poems such as "Faction," "Petite fin du monde," "Cage d'oiseau," and "Accompagnement" take us back to the very sources of this poetry and leave us in no doubt as to the direction of the journey. But the poet has not yet renounced technique: he continues to be preoccupied with the formal perfection of a Mozart, and he retains his interest in structure. He does not venture at this point to proffer the cry which is, as we learn from the *Journal*, the only adequate expression of his inward struggle, of his desire for the absolute.

The poems which I have just mentioned are of great beauty and are sufficient in themselves to place Saint-Denys-Garneau amongst the handful of our authors whose achievement has a universal value. But I am now convinced that in *Regards et jeux dans l'espace* he did not reach the limit of his powers and that his work takes on that special quality of illumination which is the mark of complete fruition only in those poems which were written in the heat of inspiration and which he was not able to polish into perfectly balanced compositions—not because he did not have the time, but because in their spontaneity they expressed with so much force and truth the innermost convictions of his soul that he could not have retouched them without lying. The emotions which he had revealed with the utmost discretion in *Regards et jeux dans l'espace* had been so little understood that he considered himself barred from uttering cries of undisguised savagery in polite society—the cries of a wounded beast, the cries of a man who in an agony of self-denunciation is crushed by the absolute.

In two-thirds of the posthumous poems, all distance is abolished between the inward experience and its outward expression. No longer are there images of life, but life itself; no longer are there symbols, but acts. No longer do we have to ask ourselves the meanings of words in order to participate in a momentous spiritual drama: the words have become flesh and soul and make the intangible tangible for us, the invisible visible.

Time and space no longer exist, and no longer must we pass from one moment to another, from one place to another. Everything is the immediate present: it is the destiny of man with his infinite capacities which is revealed at a single stroke. Images are condensed to the point where one word suffices to tell all, and commentary becomes redundant. We join in the cry that bares the soul, the illumination that lights up the whole of human destiny. In this context the poetry of Saint-Denys-Garneau takes its place with the great voices of our time. Closer to the poetry of Bernanos and Malraux than that of some poets of the same period, it blends with the anguish of today's poets. It stands beyond surrealism,

which has remained foreign to it. It poses the question of life or
death which existentialism was to take up with an insistence
bordering on mania: Can we establish communication with the
"astonishing reality" and with our fellow men? In short, is love
possible, is life no more than an illusion?

In a poem written in a humorous vein which does little to
hide his profound anguish, Saint-Denys-Garneau tells us that the
curtain parts

> Juste à peine pour entrevoir
> La fascination de la nuit
> La splendeur du jour éternel
> L'étonnante réalité.

But what is promised us (because this is a theatre) is only an
illusion, at the very most an image of the "astonishing reality."

History was the first to declare the absurdity of life, with its
concentration camps, its superb implements of war, and the misery
which disfigures it like leprosy. Malraux, in his early novels, shows
us man advancing towards death in solitude and humiliation. A
character created by another writer whom Saint-Denys-Garneau
greatly admired, Julien Green, tells us that "le seul fait d'exister
est oppressant, et l'on ne s'y habitue, sans doute, qu'en accomplis-
sant des besognes imbéciles." A French poet, Yves Bonnefoy, has
well said:

> Je ne suis que parole intentée à l'absence,
> L'absence détruira tout mon ressassement,
> Oui, c'est bientôt périr de n'être que parole,
> Et c'est tâche fatale et vain couronnement.

And yet man refuses to quit; he gets up again and faces death
squarely. But why? Malraux, according to Gaétan Picon, replies:
in order to give birth to images powerful enough to cancel out his
nothingness. We must, then, be satisfied with a simple image of
this "astonishing reality" which is capable of replenishing us.
Bernanos and Green believe in love because they believe in Christ,
who came to confirm it. But how can we rise to this love which
alone ensures a communication of life? If they are more hopeful
than Malraux, they can still only say to us, like him, that we must
refuse to give up, and that a writer can do no better than to go on
formulating his words without remission in the void. "La perpé-

tuelle recherche de l'expression," says Bernanos, "n'est que l'image affaibli, ou comme le symbole, de la perpétuelle recherche de l'Etre." This is again to cancel out nothingness; but it is not yet to possess Being. No matter what happens, man must pass through the gate of death in solitude and humiliation.

But it is a venture which defeats the powers of language. The artist survives in his work, but this is not much consolation to him in the hour of death. And yet, who knows? If he has been able to confront death, question it, hold it in check, is this not proof that death is not omnipotent, that something in us will eternally resist it? Here, at any rate, it is an act of faith that is asked of us, and neither art nor philosophy can make it into a certainty.

The poems of Saint-Denys-Garneau, and particularly the posthumous ones, bring us to the decisive moment of human destiny which is the meeting face to face with death. At first reading, the poems express the sense of wonder we have at the earth's beauty; but this is not enough to assuage our thirst. We must go beyond, and this means entering solitude, night, and desert. The distance grows between us and the "astonishing reality" which is the object of our desire, and soon we recognize this solitude for what it truly is: death, which penetrates us right to the very marrow. To look it in the face is to challenge it, and to achieve this final lucidity, this lucidity at all costs, is to push boldness as far as it will go.

Here is a page of the *Journal* which recalls many others that are sometimes more desperate, but which seems to me to include all the elements of the tragedy:

Depuis deux jours, j'ai repris l'*Imitation* que je n'avais pas pratiquée depuis bien des mois. Ça été un émerveillement renouvelé pour mon âme. Quelle magnificence de bonté et de beauté, de justesse et de passion, passion transfigurée qu'est la charité! Force et beauté merveilleuses des images dans leur simplicité. Calme majestueux du ton dans la profondeur de la tendresse; suavité; et jusqu'au *tempo* haletant de certaines pages comme fondantes d'extase. Analogie avec *L'art de la fugue* de Bach. . . .

Il me semble bien que, au fond, le jeu est fini pour moi, l'attitude du "spectateur" contre laquelle parle aussi Gabriel Marcel dans *Etre et avoir*. Les problèmes se posent à moi d'une façon vitale, et je suis forcé de leur trouver une solution pratique qui devient de plus en plus exigeante: question de vie ou de mort; je ne puis plus en sortir. Fini le temps des solutions théoriques. Il me faut m'engager et jusqu'aux os. A vrai dire, il ne me reste plus que les os. Je n'ai pas eu la sincérité de m'engager librement, quand j'aurais pu y porter un cœur encore vivant. J'ai usé en vanités toute la chair autour des os, en vains feux d'artifice, toute la chaleur de la chair. Maintenant je suis forcé, je dois, sans chaleur, engager la carcasse. Tout la reste est déjà contre moi, moi la carcasse. Il faut m'engager.

J'ai l'impression d'être exigé actuellement par chaque problème qui se pose, de n'avoir plus le loisir de tempérer. Bonne, dure nécessité. Que Dieu me donne la grâce de pouvoir réaliser ce qu'Il veut de moi!

Saint-Denys-Garneau despairs of finding in this life that "magnificence de bonté et de beauté" which seems to him to have its source in saintliness and authentic poetry. He sees no other course but to commit himself, and commit himself to the hilt. Charity, in the sense of the offering of oneself, is no longer that transfigured emotion of light and joy, but simply a waiting—gnawed with anguish, threatened by despair. Give myself? But give what? Rather the single hope that God should take what is honest of me: the skeleton.

The Word of God is the essence of this hope, and the simple possibility of waiting; but the lassitude, the weariness, the indifference of others are enough to stifle him. It is often completely dark, and one resists without really knowing why: in truth, only the bones now resist death. Some very brief poems (mere images, which are all the more striking because of their simplicity) allow us to share in these ultimate moments of the struggle:

> Quand on est réduit à ses os
> Assis sur ses os
> Couché en ses os
> Avec la nuit devant soi.

One step backwards and he will sink into nothingness. Sometimes he is there, standing as it were in front of himself in the black night:

> Et cependant dressé en nous
> Un homme qu'on ne peut pas abattre
>
> ....
> Debout en os et les yeux fixés sur le néant
> Dans une effroyable confrontation obstinée et un défi.

87

It is the complete stripping away to essentials that gives to the question of life and death its full reality, to all acts of life their full sense of urgency. Here is the close embrace of man and woman that takes us back to the origins of the human race, or into the depths of the subconscious:

> Sous le ciel rouge de mes paupières
> Les montagnes
> Sont des compagnes de mes bras
> Et les forêts qui brûlent dans l'ombre
> Et les animaux sauvages
> Passant aux griffes de tes doigts
> O mes dents
> Et toute la terre mourante étreinte
> Puis le sang couvrant la terre
> Et les secrets brûlés vifs
> Et tous les mystères déchirés
> Jusqu'au dernier cri la nuit est rendue.

Set amidst the fires of these exalted images, the unexpected exclamation "O mes dents" expresses all the savagery of the world, just as the last line, "Jusqu'au dernier cri la nuit est rendue," expresses the supreme desire of the spirit—this last cry which man yields up when all secrets have been burned alive and all mysteries torn apart.

One sentence of the *Journal* leads us to the very extremity of hope:

Je suis rompu, brisé, pulvérisé. Il ne reste plus rien que ce devoir insupportable en moi qui ne me laisse pas de repos, de cette espèce de repos de tout lâcher, de m'abandonner, tous muscles desserrés, au désespoir, à rien, à rien; dormir, dormir, ce dernier devoir d'espérer.

No, let us not yet speak of illness. What has been said is true because death exists. And it is not necessary to go back to prehistoric times to be convinced of the savagery of the struggle for life; it seems to me that the wars of our times save us the trouble. But the ultimate proof of the authenticity of this experience is to be found, in my opinion, in the beauty of the verse—as also in the beauty of the few lines of prose I have just quoted.

It is beauty which delivers us from Shakespeare's monsters, which makes us applaud at the end of his horrible stories and lets us leave the theatre with a smile on our lips, happier and better than we were when we went in. And these monsters, welling up from prehistory or the subconscious, are perhaps only images of a very real monster which is neither behind us nor beneath the level of our consciousness, but in front of us: death. Beauty defeats death. It does not eliminate it, but it holds it at a respectful distance, just far enough removed for us to fulfil our destiny, and, I am sure, to discover within ourselves a way which permits us to run the course without perishing. To the extent that the expression is beautiful ("happy," as we say) the fear of death is surmounted, and all anguish. Light is born of our self-realization, and life becomes possible, even if death is not definitively conquered. The powers of art, however, cannot guarantee us this victory; the final stage of our salvation requires us to cross the threshold into faith.

Art can lead us to this threshold, and the poetry of Saint-Denys-Garneau does this. And I must remark here that the more the presence of death intrudes, and the more its threat grows, the more assured the expression becomes, the broader the rhythm, the more striking the word, the more numerous and profound the themes. Tolstoi tells us that recognition of death is the precondition of lucidity. While still very young, Saint-Denys-Garneau was stripped of those desires which are only reflections of the real and which we so easily mistake for reality; all the veils were torn aside and he was confronted with his destiny.

In his last poems he will need only a single word to say everything, but he will also be able to say everything without obscuring what cannot be named. The great and simple words which sum up the whole of human destiny and which lead us to the threshold of faith take on here their full meaning and become a summons to what lies beyond. The same words in the hands of superficial poets are no more than pale images of reality. Birth and death, love and absence, night and light are, in this poetry of Saint-Denys-Garneau, acts which solicit our participation, and not merely symbols which invite reflection. It is likewise at the most decisive moments of challenge that his prose becomes most luminous. Not only does the word gain in precision, but the sentence reproduces in all its subtlety the unexpected development of his feeling. It is action—not just a simple reflection of reality, but drama.

Whenever I reread the *Journal* of Saint-Denys-Garneau, the

quality of the language captures and astonishes me more each time. And always the quality seems to me firmer and more authoritative in the more direct and spontaneous passages—those in which there is hardly any interval between the feeling and its expression, between the emotion of anguish and the language which is the soul's reply. The accent is vigorous and the inspiration rich. A sentence of as much as ten lines, for example, in which the thought unfolds at the extreme limits of the imaginable will avoid confusion even in its complexity. It is composed of words which seem to be uttered for the first time, and the voice is steady right to the end, which is at the same time a new point of departure. Anguish is very near at hand, but well under control, almost tamed. This victory of poetry, from which the poet, alas, could not benefit, is found throughout the *Journal*. For this narrative, loosely composed as each day goes by, takes on the form of the most polished of poems. There is the beginning, with its moments of enthusiasm and distress, then the account of the horrible spring and summer days of 1937, when the drama reveals its essence, and finally the great meditations on renunciation, grief, and poverty which look towards a far-off light shining in the darkness and lend a meaning to the silence following the cries of horror in the last poems.

If so much greatness appears in this misery, it is because the *Journal* puts us in touch with a man who has suffered more than we have, but who has followed a road familiar to those who sometimes dare to probe their inner beings. And his presence provides us with an answer to our worst agonies because it springs up in our solitude like a sure friend. Thus we learn for the first time something about ourselves that the moralists cannot teach us, something which completely expresses our inner reality.

The intimate pages of the *Journal,* then, are linked with the poems which were born during the same painful years between 1935 and 1939. I know of no other poetry in which death is more cruelly present, nor of any, perhaps, in which life, wounded and condemned, tears from silence a more moving proof of the majesty of man's destiny.

Saint-Denys-Garneau truly reaches the depths of anguish and love where man's drama begins. But here again, because the poem is an offering and a communication, anguish is necessarily ex-

90

pressed in a burst of fraternal feeling; and it leads us, by the very fact that it is given in poetic form, if not to man's immediate redemption, at least to a promise of joy. Certainly there are times when death comes and breaks the impetus of love, and the poet knows the terror of absence; but, dissatisfied with himself, he lives through each moment of the agony. In the reader's case, life and aesthetic insight mitigate the cries of terror and permit him to escape from an otherwise overwhelming sense of solitude: however devastating the final visions may be, the poem remains; it always moves us, and thus we escape the death it evokes.

For the expression to be to this extent forceful, for the verse or the sentence to remain inseparable from the inner experience at the core, and for both to reach us as an experience and not as a simple reflection, all illusion had to disappear, desire had to be outstripped, destiny had to be confronted in complete lucidity.

All this is undoubtedly true. And yet Saint-Denys-Garneau was ill, psychologically and physically ill. I have already said that his illness is transcended in his poetry just as his fear is, by the very beauty of the work; but as far as his day-to-day life was concerned, illness had exhausted him after four years of facing up to his destiny. Let us remember that it is a rare person who can achieve such visions without being consumed by their intensity. Since, unlike most human beings, he could not bring himself to accept the mediocrity of life, he would have needed exceptional health indeed to have continued, as he wanted to, to respond to his inner compulsions.

Saint-Denys-Garneau leads us to the limits of the humanly possible, and we know from his *Journal* that he went even farther, led by faith into the darkness. And because he had the courage that comes with clear-sightedness he lays before us his experience of maturity, the first experience of like intensity to come out of French Canada. It was, of course, not the last, and indeed it could not have been fulfilled then if the community had not been mysteriously ready to welcome it.

I believe that the great economic crisis of the thirties made all nationalistic and conservative rhetoric suddenly seems so hollow, made traditions whose origins were lost in the mists of the past seem so empty, made the prejudices of a society which allowed millions of men to wallow in misery and ignorance seem so childish, that salvation had now to be sought in the future rather than in the past. The world already knew that it was being threatened by death and that it was necessary to chart new routes at all costs. Every phase of life was re-examined—and there were some at least who refused to shut their eyes to the facts.

If by virtue of courage and clarity of vision a work of great maturity was born at precisely that moment, it could only be the sign of the beginning of a renewal, the sign of a transition to an age of maturity. The road is long and winding, particularly in a world without frontiers, and especially for a French-speaking community within an Anglo-Saxon continent. The creative arts have given other signs of maturing, and it matters little that failures have had to be admitted in other fields. There have been writers such as Gabrielle Roy, Anne Hébert, and André Langevin; there has also been the liberation of painting—and I am thinking of Borduas especially, who is another poet scorched by his meeting with death and who in his last canvases, as in Saint-Denys-Garneau's last poems, in spite of solitude and illness, has attained to the full mastery of his gifts, to a nobility of matter and a stark simplicity of style, to a vigour of expression whose strength is a faultless clarity of vision.

It is on Canadian soil that these works affirming maturity are born, in the heart of a reality which, whether we wish it or not, unites English-speaking and French-speaking Canadians. On that plane all spiritual contacts are possible, and it is on that plane alone that a close relationship can be developed. We owe a great debt to those who have the courage to start from the beginning, to put all things to the question, even life itself, in order to dissipate the lie that veils the wonder of reality. Saint-Denys-Garneau had that courage.

J. W. DAFOE

J. W. Dafoe was in every sense a self-made man. He was born in 1866 near Combermere, a village in the county of Renfrew, not far from Ottawa. It was hardly a village, there being only a bridge over the Madawaska river with a few log houses on either side. His father, Calvin, was a farmer of sorts but all who lived in this area made their living from the lumber trade. Dafoe's uncle, Edwin Elcome, who lived at nearby Arnprior, was a boss of lumber operations and often took his nephew to spend a week-end in one of the rough shanties. In later years, when a reminiscent mood came upon him, Dafoe could summon up memories of the shanty-man's life, of the skill of the river drivers, of his father wresting a knife from the hand of a drunken attacker, or of a man, whose name at this stage escaped him, being mauled to death by a bear. Dafoe had the physical strength for the life of a lumberjack but not the desire or aptitude. He was more comfortable with a pen in his hand than with an axe—with a book rather than a bottle. Books were scarce and he read anything he could lay his hands on, his chief supply being a cache he discovered in an abandoned shack that had once been the property of an Irish schoolmaster. His brother Cal, when asked recently why Jack went into journalism, replied simply, "Well, he was no good around the place." His mother arranged for him to live with relatives and attend high school in Arnprior; he led his class and a year before his death recalled this achievement as the most completely satisfying one of his life. At the age of fifteen he organized the first school at Egan Estate Settlement, or Murchison, as it is now known, and became its first teacher, continuing in that role until his age was discovered and it was suggested to him that he should still be attending rather than teaching school. His sister Edith remembers him at this time and writes: "When he came home at Christmas 1882 he was a man in size . . . he looked a big ruffian to us . . . he had bought himself clothes out of the shanty-man's storehouse and a gorgeous tam-o'-shanter to cover his bright red hair."

How did this boy from the backwoods transform himself into the dean of Canadian editors? How did he equip his mind with the knowledge to debate the future of the Empire with the Fellows of All Souls College and to influence its development as a confidant of Sir Robert Borden at Versailles in 1919 and of Mackenzie King at the Imperial Conference of 1923? The process began in 1883 when, by answering an advertisement, Dafoe got a job as a cub reporter with the *Montreal Star*. P. D. Ross, the chief editorial writer, gave him help and encouragement. Edmund O'Connor, the managing editor and a kindly, even-tempered man, sensed the potential of the boy's mind and pushed him along in the reporter's trade. At first there was difficulty; Dafoe was, as O'Connor put it later, too green. But, as frequently happened later in his career, the qualities he happened to have were just the ones needed. The *Star* was building up a case against a clothing store on St. Joseph Street, near Bonaventure Station, whose salesmen were picking up country bumpkins and lumberjacks as they got off the train, enticing them into the store, selling them expensive suits and substituting very cheap ones in the parcels taken home. At least this is what O'Connor suspected, but he needed proof. Dafoe was to be used as a decoy; he recalled the incident later:

They equipped me with an old-fashioned green travelling bag; I did not have to put on any old clothes because I had them already. I went down to the station on circus day and wandered down St. Joseph Street carrying the bag and looking around at the wonder of Montreal. I was picked up at once. The next week they started to expose the store, on the second day the paper was sued for libel and the third day my story appeared in all its glory. It blew up the libel suit; it blew up the store, and it blew the swindlers

94

out of Montreal. . . . Now that was not a bad start for a country boy.

Six months later the *Star* sent him to the Press Gallery in Ottawa. Afternoons and evenings were spent listening to the debates and writing dispatches. Mornings were spent in the alcoves of the parliamentary library. His older and more experienced colleagues began to be aware of him when, by luck, he got hold of the casualty list of the North-West Rebellion a few hours in advance of his competitors. In 1885 he left the *Star* to be editor of the newly launched *Ottawa Journal*, but, since he was only nineteen, the job was too much for him and he resigned after six months to go with the *Manitoba Free Press* as an editorial writer and reporter. He stayed with this job for nearly seven years and entered with gusto into the life of the frontier, playing lacrosse, rowing on the Assiniboine, riding horseback over the prairie in summer, curling and skating in winter, and talking politics with his cronies continually. In 1888 he was one of a group that went out to Fort Whyte to put a crossing over the C.P.R. line—by force if necessary. The C.P.R. had refused right of way to the provincial line being built to the border and the group who went were spoiling for a fight. They were disappointed when the C.P.R. called off its men and took the case to court. Another incident which Dafoe remembered with some pride arose when his life was threatened by a saloon-keeper. The bartender had been supplementing his income by matching his belligerent bulldog against all comers. Dafoe reported one such match in the paper with the names of all found-ins, with the result that all concerned were indicted before a Grand Jury. The gang swore revenge and the Chief of Police equipped the reporter with a Smith and Wesson revolver, but it was never necessary to use it.

In 1890 Dafoe returned to Ottawa for what was, perhaps, the most significant event of his life—his marriage to Alice Parmlee. Words are inadequate to convey the tenderness of the relationship between them, the warmth of family life that developed. Two quotations from letters may give some idea. Eleven years after they were married, Dafoe stumbled on a bundle of love-letters written when they were engaged and after rereading them wrote his wife, who was visiting relatives: "It was like looking in a glass and seeing not the rotund and commonplace visage of 35 but the eager and nervous features of a boy. But though my style now has a soberer line the love of husband and father needs not to borrow inspiration from the passion of youth: in my case ... my dreams came true and the reality differed from the imagining only to transcend it." The couple lived in Winnipeg until 1893 and then went to Montreal when Dafoe went with the *Herald* and then became editor of Hugh Graham's *Weekly Star*. In 1901 he became editor of the *Manitoba Free Press* and came to Winnipeg two months in advance of the family. The following quotation comes from a letter he wrote Mrs. Dafoe in September, 1910, just before he returned to bring them back to the new house on Spence Street:

After I got the fires started I spent some time fixing up my bookcases— and some day dreaming about the joy the immediate future has for me. I set the clock going and can hear its cheerful tick-tock in the next room ... I think you will like the electric light; it is so bright, clean and safe ... I am not very busy at the office; in fact I am not in trim for work being as excited as a small boy who counts the days until Christmas ... were I a cold-blooded methodical business man I would stop over in Ottawa on my way down ... but thank heaven I am not cold blooded: when I leave here I shall go straight to you and shall count every hour until I can see you with my eyes and hold you in my arms.

Love of family, magnanimity, a powerful mind, immense physical energy—these were characteristics Dafoe had by nature. Environment had foisted others on him, some of which had to be overcome or moderated. His family background was Orange Protestantism; "the 12th of July," his sister wrote, "was second only to Christmas in our house." The alchemy of experience and reading transformed this inheritance into a practical Christianity and a hatred of dogma in all its forms. In 1906 he wrote:

I don't think there was ever a more damnable doctrine preached than that we are all lost souls to be saved only by faith in creeds supplemented by a certain measure of good deeds, this is the pestilential root from which all the black fruits of clericalism have sprouted— the pretence of holding the keys of heaven, the persecutions hellish in their ferocity, the demand of the church to control men's lives and opinions ... I have no creed but I do try to follow a long way off and with stumbling footsteps the example of the Master—to be as kind as I can, and as honest as I can, to live not altogether to myself, to love my fellow men.... It is a system that I manage to live by after a fashion, and I can die by it too when the time comes sooner or later.

J. W. Dafoe's family were Tory, but he became very much a partisan Liberal, influenced, so legend has it, by a speech of Edward Blake's made in 1885 in the House of Commons. Certainly his partisanship plus journalistic ability earned him his appointment as editor of Clifford Sifton's *Manitoba Free Press*. For some years his activities were largely oriented to the welfare of the party. The paper in 1901 was a centre for the distribution of patronage. Dafoe addressed political meetings, attended nomination conventions, wrote propaganda to be translated into Ukrainian and German, and generally participated in backroom activities of all kinds.

It took many years to outgrow this role of journalistic servant of the party and to remove a stigma like the one Goldsmith pressed on Burke when he wrote:

> Who, born for the universe, narrow'd his mind,
> And to party gave up what was meant for mankind.

Bitter partisanship was gradually transformed into a philosophy of liberalism which was basically nineteenth century in its outlook. While the great game of politics continued to fascinate until the day of his death, political choice often lay between "something bad and something not much better." He admitted to Grattan O'Leary in 1928 that he was a Liberal because "there are less sons of bitches in the Liberal party than in the Tory." One may challenge the count and still appreciate the candour.

The editorship of the *Free Press* was in some ways confining, but it also made possible a good deal of travel and a chance for Dafoe to see the sites of historical events he was always reading about. In 1906 he represented the Canadian Press at the Congress of International Chambers of Commerce in Milan, Italy. The trip took him first to Britain, where he took time off for a trip through the Highlands of Scotland, starting at Edinburgh: "I had read volumes about Edinburgh," he wrote, "but found my preconceived ideas all wrong."

He could not understand why there should be a monument "commemorating and lauding that Royal Lobster the Duke of York who because he was George III's son was commander of the

army a hundred years ago." As a Canadian he had high standards
for natural beauty. It was, he felt, the glamour and romance of
historical association and not the physical settings that made the
Highlands interesting.

London, where he stayed at the Russell Hotel, was a rare combination of historic sites, interesting personalities, and the theatre.
He called on Lord Strathcona, who, at the age of 86, he found
"able to outwork most of the men in his office." Hamar Greenwood, a young Canadian barrister and member of the House of
Commons for York, introduced him to some of the local celebri-
ties, among them Winston Churchill, whom he described as "able,
aggressive and slightly impudent." They went to the House of
Lords, but J. W. was not impressed. "Lord Dundonald," he wrote,
"who made such a mess of things in Canada, was laying down the
law and pounding the desk." Greenwood and his shaggy guest
beat a hasty retreat to Westminster Abbey. A two-day visit to
Paris corresponded with the anniversary of the fall of the Bastille,
and Dafoe stayed up nearly all night watching the street-dancing.
He arrived at Milan on July 17, 1906, and went immediately to
the Congress he was to report and the Canadian exposition: "It
did me good," he wrote, "to see Canadian faces and hear the
Canadian brand of speech again." A few days later he recorded:
"Have also reformed my diet. Instead of eating the messes they
dish up here I go to good restaurants and order civilized dishes
... went to Cova's last night ... ordered a steak with potatoes and
peas: got them to brew me a pot of tea; demanded butter with my
bread: and with a dish of soup and some good cheese I made a very
satisfactory snack."

Dafoe was a most thorough tourist. He did not stop at the level
of the guide-books, but read his history assiduously and visited and
examined everything of significance. In Italy it was art; none of
the main galleries on his route were missed; "it is really the desire
to see Raphael's Madonnas," he wrote, "that is drawing me to
Florence, of all the paintings I have seen his are the ones that
seem to me most wonderful." The trip in 1906 was hurried and
did little more than whet an appetite which was partially satisfied
in 1909, when he went to the Imperial Press Conference in London. All the pomp, circumstance, pageantry, and power of the
heart of the Empire was brought to bear on the Conference. The

week of June 1 was typical: mornings were occupied by official business, which meant that the group gathered in the big room of the foreign office in Downing Street to be addressed by such men as Sir Edward Grey, R. B. Haldane, Lord Morley, and Winston Churchill, to mention only a few. On Monday there was lunch at the House of Commons followed by a garden party on the lawn of Marlborough House, where the group were presented to the King and Queen. In the evening Lord Derby gave a dinner, and this was followed by a reception at the home of the Marquis of Salisbury. Tuesday afternoon there was a trip to Sutton Place (Lord Northcliffe's home), where Dafoe for the first time met Moberly Bell, the business manager of the *Times,* and had a long conversation with Lord Roberts. On Wednesday there was the Lord Mayor's luncheon at the Mansion House with "dinner off gold plate and all that sort of thing." Thursday he attended the Conservative Club lunch, a garden party at Apsley House, had dinner with Lord Northcliffe, and went to a reception at Stafford House given by the Duke and Duchess of Sutherland.

On Friday there was the usual review of the fleet at Portsmouth: "The trip through the Navy was the greatest spectacle I ever expect to see. There were 144 warships embracing some 7 or 8 of the Dreadnought type, and the lines in 4 parallel columns covered 18 miles." Britain and the Empire were hard to resist in those days, and there is some evidence that Dafoe was temporarily swept off his feet as Laurier had been at the Diamond Jubilee. The *Sheffield Daily Telegraph* reported a speech at the Lord Mayor's lunch as follows:

Mr. J. W. Dafoe responded in a strikingly able speech. He remarked that the delegates were all British by birth or by descent and, coming back to England, they had been made to understand that they were not distant relations but that they were indeed in their mother's house with their brothers and sisters all about them. "You have your party divisions here," he said, "as we have at home but in Imperial questions there are no party divisions."

There were no more trips abroad until the Peace Conference in Paris ten years later. Dafoe continued to broaden himself by very wide reading—Greek classics, political biography, poetry, and many of the happy-ending type of books on liberalism. George Iles, a person who is somewhat shrouded in mystery, but who appears to have been a hotel hermit in New York, was continually ransacking the second-hand bookstores on the editor's behalf. At least once a year Dafoe renewed his political and journalistic contacts in Ottawa, Washington, and New York. Each time he went to New York he went to the latest plays, and usually to the Authors' Club, the Metropolitan Museum, and the Museum of Natural History. He was particularly fond of good music; within two days in November, 1911, for example, he heard Zimbalist, a famous Russian violinist, at Carnegie Hall, the New York Philharmonic in a Wagnerian concert at the same place, the choir at Grace Church, and, as he wrote Mrs. Dafoe, "I travelled the whole length of New York to hear an organ recital at the College of the City of New York. It was very fine—the great features being the overture to Lohengrin and Bach's great Toccata."

In 1919 Sir Robert Borden invited Dafoe to attend the Peace Conference in Paris as the representative of the Canadian press in the British press delegation. This conference had an immense influence on his later thinking. He sailed from New York in late November, 1918; Clifford Sifton was also on board, and editor and publisher spent the voyage swapping books and stories. Dafoe lent Sifton *Joan and Peter* by H. G. Wells and found that it suited his chief perfectly:

... during his stay in England he had acquired admiration for the capacity and staying power of the common people and a large contempt for the ruling class... Wells' furious biting attack on all typical English institutions, church and school, social hierarchy and governing machinery, marched with his mood and he chortled over every page ... Wells' dislike of Victorianism I can understand though I do not fully share it; but why should he refer to Queen Victoria as "a little old panting German widow"—nothing very clever about that sort of talk.

The Canadian party arrived in London on December 3 and left for Paris just over one month later. Claridges, Dafoe found too class-conscious for him; he had his meals either in his room or at one of the restaurants nearby, very often at Holborn's, which he described as having "a series of dining rooms of varying degrees of style—the grill room for sensible old chaps like me who mostly want something to eat." Christmas he spent with his son Jack and with Grant Dexter, both of whom were on leave from their units, and New Year's Eve he stationed himself at a strategic point in Piccadilly Circus to watch the crowds. Paris was a real challenge, both from the point of view of the Peace Conference and that of the city itself. The picture of Dafoe that emerges is that of the self-made man stolidly continuing his education, reading French history at night and plotting a route to walk over and explore at the first opportunity. He became a kind of unofficial guide to the Canadian party; early in February he recorded in his diary:

... yesterday I constituted myself an amateur guide for old Paris and the victims seemed to enjoy it. There was Col. Ralston who is here from the front and Billy Banks of the Toronto Globe.... We went by underground to Place de la Bastille and walked from there to Place Vendome taking in Hotel de Ville, Notre Dame, Pont Neuf, Rue Honoré, Palais Royal and Church of St. Roch. I retailed the local knowledge I have been acquiring.

A few days later he took Ralston to Versailles and found that the official guide told some whopping lies. The Palace itself he considered ample justification for the revolution.

Then of course there were the people attending the Peace Conference, the full sessions which the press could attend, and the private briefing from Sir Robert Borden. The list of people Dafoe met reads like an international *Who's Who*: Lawrence of Arabia, Chaim Weizmann, Sir George Ridell, Lionel Curtis, Philip Kerr, Smuts, Botha, Sir Maurice Hanky, General Currie (who arranged a tour of the battlefields), Oscar Strauss, the head of the American League of Nations movement, not to mention a whole galaxy of the best-known editors and journalists of the day. All these plus the Conference itself had a profound influence on Dafoe; he wrote: "I see most—not all—the secret documents relating to the conference and they contain all kinds of first class news which I cannot use. I am like an old toper in a room full of drink but forbidden to take a drop. However I'll know the inside history of this conference which will be very much worth while."

Dafoe got back to London *en route* home on March 8, his fifty-fourth birthday. What kind of man was he at this stage, and what was his situation in life? He had progressed from a backwoods hick to a man of immense if unsystematic knowledge. He had gone

101

from cub reporter to an editor of great national prestige and considerable international standing. Moreover, he had acquired that most rare and precious of all editorial privileges—complete independence and freedom to use his judgement. True, there was a large measure of agreement between publisher and editor, but where it was lacking the editor's opinions prevailed; in fact, the editor had become the paper, and for the next twenty-four years he exercised a substantial influence on Canadian history.

This influence and the opinions, principles, and philosophy from which it sprang may be examined under three descriptive headings: liberalism, nationalism, and internationalism. Dafoe's *Free Press* became known as a great liberal journal, a kind of Canadian *Manchester Guardian* that attempted to apply nineteenth-century liberal doctrine to twentieth-century Canada. No such simple statement as this can convey an accurate impression of the mind and faith of the editor. It is doubtful if he ever tried to work out a political philosophy for himself; had he done so he would certainly have added the words "pragmatic" and "realist" to the word "liberal." He was much too good a journalist and too close an observer of human affairs to accept any *clichés* about the rationality of man; selfishness, not rationality, was, as he saw it, the basic human characteristic, and life was a race between education and disaster. *Laissez faire* was justified only if it was combined with free trade; but entrenched behind a tariff, it "appeals to greed, selfishness, the sense of national superiority and most of the other wretched weaknesses of human nature."

He found it easier to state what he was against rather than what he was for. The two things he was most against were Toryism and socialism, but it must be admitted that he defined these philosophies so as to make his opposition dramatic. A Tory, to Dafoe, was one who believed in a class society in which privileged positions were protected by the state, a colonial-minded person rather scornful of Canada's accomplishments and anxious to link up with centres of power and influence in London. After the election of 1911 Dafoe wrote George Iles:

The fact is, as I have long known, Canada is now and has been for a generation an essentially Tory country. That is to say, the right of corporations, moneyed interests, etc., to determine the policy of the country is recognized by the majority of the electors. Laurier achieved office in 1896 mainly through a series of blunders by his opponents, supplemented by their loss, in rapid succession, of able men; and upon obtaining office he held it for a long period of time by placating various powerful interests at the expense of the general public. The moment he showed signs of putting real Liberal doctrine into effect, the interests combined and crushed him. I should be well content to see the Liberal party remain in opposition for the next fifteen or twenty years, if it will devote itself to advocating real Liberal views and building a party which, when it again takes office, will be able to carry out a programme without regard to the desires and feelings of the privileged classes.

The party was out of office for a decade and it is therefore fair to ask what Dafoe advocated for it when it came back. He fought hard to avoid domination by "predatory eastern financial interests" and the "clericism of Quebec." But there is some evidence that he considered true liberalism as possible only on an agrarian base and among the honest folk of the western plains; he was often unsympathetic to organized labour and was always unwilling to face the implications of controlling the "predatory capitalists" in Montreal and Toronto. His editorials and correspondence are full of such phrases as the following: "the business of liberalism everywhere is to work to bring about the conditions which would make possible the largest possible exercise of individual talent free from anti-social practices"; or (in 1933) "the vindication of the principle that industrial and financial power should be held accountable for its social effects might become forthwith a policy for liberalism. There might indeed be a searching of hearts as to why this objective has not already been achieved." But how was it to be achieved? Certainly not by an extension of state action because this might lead to socialism.

Dafoe was unduly frightened by the word "socialism," partly because, for purposes of his hard-hitting editorials, he insisted on defining it in its most extreme form. "As a practical policy," he wrote by way of comment on the Regina Manifesto,

Socialism and Communism are the same thing, the divergence is with respect to the tactics by which the obliteration of individualism and the transforming of men into ants can best be brought about. The Communists are all for bloody revolution and the dictatorship of the proletariat, while the socialists hope to gain the same ends by more ordinary means.

This equation of Marxist communism, British Labour Party socialism, and dictatorship frightened him out of his rationality;
indeed he often wrote about the Labour Party as if Hyndman's
Social Democratic Federation had succeeded rather than failed.

In 1931 the top Liberals of Canada gathered at Vincent Mas-
sey's home in Port Hope to chart a course for the future. Dafoe
submitted his ideas: "the first essential," he wrote, "is that the
party make an end once and for all to the long established custom
of trying by compromising its principles to retain within the party
men enamoured of Tory performances." The tariff must be re-
stored at least to where it was before Bennett took office; Canada
must have a Central Bank with some control over credit. ("Don't
ask the professional bankers about this," he warned, "they know
nothing of the machinery they operate.") The independence and
integrity of the C.N.R. must be guaranteed so as to protect the
community against "powerful and designing special interests."
Finally, the party should sponsor proportional representation.

This was a pretty meagre programme to meet the depression,
and Dafoe knew it. He was discouraged and confused by the depression, the American New Deal, British protectionism, and the
rise of Fascism in Europe. In February, 1931, when he was in
Nassau writing the life of Clifford Sifton, he wrote a friend: "the
masses and underdogs are getting the idea firmly fixed in their
noodles that the existing system, financial and industrial . . . has
got to look after their needs under pain of being smashed up. The
inability of our system to do this is demonstrated from time to
time by these recurrent depressions. . . . Liberalism is shrunken
from a great host to a handful of prophets—prophesying doom—
like myself." On New Year's Day, 1934, he wrote Harry Sifton
offering to resign as editor; the theories of deficit financing, pump-
priming, and all the ideas of "the monetary magicians and miracle
men" were getting him down. He thought a young man might do
better, but he ended the letter with: "I spent a hard day yesterday
with Keynes' Treatise on Money reading it not admiringly but
critically in the mood to give him an occasional kick in the behind
. . . he is rather stimulating."

Dafoe was primarily a crusading editor who loved a battle to
fight and an attack to be mounted. The most satisfying battle he
fought was on the issue of Canadian nationhood and autonomous

status within the Empire. He was the most consistent and forceful exponent of Canadian nationalism of his time or any other time. The vision and eloquence of D'Arcy McGee was stilled by an assassin's bullet. Joseph Howe had spent himself before Confederation. W. A. Foster, who in 1871 used those famous words, "unless we intend to be hewers of wood and drawers of water until the end we should in right earnest set about the strengthening the foundations of our identity," found that the Canada First movement had collapsed four years after he founded it. Bourassa's energies were spent largely in regional nationalism, and John S. Ewart weakened his case by overstatement. Dafoe's background was just right: how different he would have been if he had been born in Toronto and gone to Upper Canada College and thence to Trinity. How different he would have been if he had read some history before experiencing it. His mind, which had great native, indigenous power, might have acquired humility and subtlety; he might have been less dogmatic in his opinions, less able to indulge in sledge hammer attacks on those who stood in the way of ends he thought desirable. But he would have been less colourful and less memorable.

Much of the combined energy, political instinct and personal conviction of the *Free Press*'s owner and editor focused for twenty-five years on the question of Canadian nationhood. They rode the issue in tandem, each urging the other on. If there were ever any doubts about their stand, the Alaska Boundary dispute of 1903 dispelled them. Clifford Sifton, as Minister of the Interior, handled Canada's case and found dealings with the British most unsatisfactory. As Sifton saw it, Canadian representations were ignored; Lord Alverstone, the British delegate on the commission created to settle the dispute, ratted on Canada; the country was little more than a pawn in a diplomatic deal between Britain and the United States. Years later Dafoe wrote, in a biography of Sifton, that the Alaska Boundary dispute was the real beginning of nationalism in Canada. This judgment may be questioned, but it certainly made the proprietor of the *Free Press* into a red-hot nationalist.

Very shortly after Dafoe became editor of the *Free Press*, the Duke and Duchess of York toured Canada. The paper argued that the Colonial Office had too much say in the tour and the

Canadian government too little, and the editor boycotted the committee in Winnipeg on which he had been put to help make the arrangements. He did join the welcoming party, and wrote of it:

at ten o'clock we started for the station—four of us to a carriage. My companions were three of the head Tories of these parts ... we created quite a dash going down Main Street—some fifteen carriages filled with plug-hatted gentlemen. I took quite a shine to the Duchess. Her photographs by no means do her justice. I should call her a good looking woman.

At the reception later, he met Lord Minto, the Governor General, but by no means took a shine to him; in fact he hurried back to the office and wrote a strong editorial, for which Laurier chided him later, on Minto's misconception of his position in Canada. Forty years later, a friend sent him a long memorandum that Minto had written on his conception of the office of the Governor General, and Dafoe wrote in acknowledging it, "I burned with humiliation at this recital of our past humiliation." Governors General were one of his favourite editorial targets throughout his career and, even though he understood very well the constitutional basis of the office, he never admitted it; the office became a symbol of an unsatisfactory relationship with Britain.

Of course many found the relationship unsatisfactory, but Dafoe had a particular intensity of feeling. He had an intense pride in Canada, a great faith in the country's potential, and an immense frustration with the slow growth of national feeling. He wrote perhaps a hundred editorials scolding Canadians on their lack of pride, their divided loyalty, and what he called their "colonialism."

The educational system was, he felt, all wrong in that too little Canadian history was taught:

The trouble in Canada is that the emphasis on national life has never been placed where it should have been placed—at home. We have never had enough national spirit to provide ourselves with a distinctive Canadian flag, we have people in Canada objecting to standing up when O Canada is sung, we have trifled with the question of citizenship and nationality.

Nothing irritated him more than the refusal of the census authorities to accept the term "Canadian" as an identification of racial origin. He scoffed at the explanation that sparse population was an excuse for the slow growth of a body of Canadian literature:

If Canada is in their bones and hearts our authors will write Canadian books ... a writer must feel intensely all the influences of environment and heredity out of which the subjects of his book emerge. Sky, soil, climate, people; a man or a family or a community at work amid surroundings peculiar to themselves, surroundings which mould habit and form character. . . . It is such books we want in Canada.

Dafoe had a lot of fun in his columns with what he called the "colonial Canadians." Howard Ferguson was described as "that blatant fire-eating ass who can only interpret the Imperial tie in terms of Canadian inferiority. No inferiority, no tie." R. B. Bennett, in this context, was seen as a "talkative opinionated treason smeller. His ideal for the Canada of today and tomorrow is the colonial relationship." The *Toronto Globe* he termed "old, deaf, dumb and blind," and the *Mail and Empire* "the organ of the congenital die-hards, the 33rd degree loyalists of Toronto." The Liberal party itself did not escape his censure; he found the resolutions on the question of Canadian autonomy passed at the 1919 convention too vague; there was too much "viewing with alarm" and too much "pointing with pride." When W. S. Fielding criticized Borden's insistence on Canadian signature of the Peace Treaty, Dafoe poured out a torrent of scalding words; Fielding, he said, was a little Canadian, a Toronto Tory; he had renounced his birthright as a political descendant of Laurier. In 1928 the Canadian and British Prime Ministers made conflicting statements about the Anglo-Egyptian Treaty negotiations; most newspapers in Canada assumed that the British statement was correct. Dafoe searched frantically for the facts, and when it turned out that King had been accurate he gleefully reviewed the statements of his fellow editors, concluding,

Can it not be taken for granted that a Canadian holding high office is as much predisposed toward telling the truth as public men in any other country? Are Canadians who are so anxious to befoul their own nest real Canadians, who are willing to stand up for Canada, or are they a collection of second-rate people calling themselves Canadians but intellectually and emotionally divorced from the country?

Canadians who were for a centralized Empire were seen either as the victims of excessive sentimentalism or as anxious to link up with a centre of power and culture outside Canada and hence confer a mark of superiority on themselves.

There was another aspect to Dafoe's thought on autonomy. Not only did the forces of North American environment make it inevitable that Canada should go her separate way, but also his personal views on the nature of a good society made this course seem desirable. He wanted Canada to be free of the dead weight of custom, prejudice, and class attitudes that he had observed in Britain and Europe. He had in 1920 a distrust of what he called the "European mind," a feeling of North American fastness and security, an appreciation of material prosperity, a belief that the spirit of the Old Adam was, in many ways, peculiar to Britain and the continent. He returned from Paris in 1919 completely disillusioned and disgusted with international power politics, and shortly after his return gave a speech at an annual meeting of the Editorial Association of the United States that came close to being isolationist in spirit. Throughout his life he saw Canada's future as intimately linked with that of the United States. His views on reciprocity are too well known to need repetition here. Perhaps the strong support he gave to a joint project for a St. Lawrence Seaway is not as well known. This support goes back a long way in the editorial columns but became strident in the twenties. The following excerpt from one of many editorials is quoted as an example:

In Canada we are familiar with the various bogeys which have been invented and put out on the line for the purpose of frightening timid folk. This is a scheme of the Yanks to steal our hydro-electric power. The Americans will get a right to partial control of Canadian water. Think of what happened at Panama. Beware the Greeks bearing gifts. Remember the Trojan Horse. This is the sort of stuff that is being ladled out.... The Ontario electorate has shown itself singularly susceptible to claptrap of this kind, and it would perhaps be premature to assume that it has now reached a level of intelligence that makes it immune.

The need for a high national spirit, the uniqueness of North American culture, the inevitability of close relations with the United States—these were some of the assumptions underlying Dafoe's views on autonomy. There was also an intense dislike of what he called imperialism, which made him an inveterate opponent of any ideas of imperial centralization. This attitude is

108

clearly seen in the clash, beginning about 1910 and continuing for over a decade, with the Liberal Imperialists of Britain. The Round Table group, as they called themselves, was made up of Lionel Curtis, Philip Kerr, L. S. Amery, Lord Milner, and others only slightly less well known. To them the preservation of liberal values depended on imperial solidarity. The British peoples, like the Levites of the Old Testament, were the custodians of the sacred principles of the rule of law and parliamentary government. They were the trustees of this divine inheritance, and it was the British white man's burden to preserve these things where they existed and extend them to others. The fact that much of the Empire was based on conquest and war was to them simply a reflection of the nature of the world and part of the struggle of good against evil. Self-government in a former colonial territory meant not complete independence but rather the assumptions of obligations that go with membership in a larger union. Dominion autonomy, while desirable and indeed inevitable in local matters, could never extend to foreign policy. Following the Versailles Treaty, the Round Table group made a concerted effort to achieve unity of imperial foreign policy, and their influence was considerable, as many of the members occupied high positions. Dafoe opposed this group at every turn. The Imperial record, as he read it, was indefensible. When Curtis talked about the white man's burden, Dafoe thought of slave labour in the South African mines or extraterritorial rights in China. Unity of foreign policy to him meant a policy made in London for the benefit of Britain. Cardwell, the Secretary of War in a Gladstone cabinet, once said that the true defence of the colonies was that they lived under the ægis of England. Dafoe did not find this point valid or relevant. Who was likely to attack us? The possibility of war with the United States seemed to him fantastic, and if it ever did come about it would be like a collision between a steam-roller and bulldog—hence, the less premeditation the better. Besides, much of the Empire to be protected was of no possible concern to Canada, having been acquired by conquest, ruled by arbitrary high-handed means, and retained largely for commercial reasons: Nigeria, Ashanti, Kenya, Uganda, Nyasaland, Rhodesia, Bechuanaland, Sudan, Somaliland, Zanzibar, North Borneo, Sarawak, Burma, or for that matter Suez and India. It was far better that such defensive arrangements as were necessary be accomplished under international authority. However, Dafoe was not in 1920 the advocate of collective security he later became. The publisher of the *Free Press* referred to the League of Nations as a collection of second-rate professors, and the editor wrote in 1925, "The preservation of Poland's Eastern frontier is not worth the bones of a single Canadian soldier," and two years later: "Our policy toward Europe should be one of aloofness. We Canadians would do well to have nothing to do politically with the continent of Europe. We should not entangle ourselves nor should we permit ourselves to be entangled by our political association." L. S. Amery was probably close to the mark when he complained that membership in the League of Nations was for Canada a badge of nationhood, a convenient proof of adult status, and a means of avoiding imperial commitments.

What relationship would Dafoe have prescribed between Canada, Britain, and the Empire had it been in his power to settle the question? This is a difficult question to answer because he engaged in almost no abstract speculation; all his editorials were written with the harsh realities of politics before him. In some private letters he argued that Canada would have been a better country in every way had it followed Galt's lead in 1867 and become fully independent; yet when Loring Christie in 1926 produced a memorandum advocating just this, he wrote "I do not go this far with Christie. . . . I do not think this essential to our full national status."

Yet Dafoe was hostile to the idea of any kind of centralized machinery for dealing with Commonwealth affairs, and in this respect often behaved as if he agreed with Christie's argument for independence. He attended the Imperial Conference of 1923 officially as a representative of the press but unofficially as an adviser to King. Of course he was against centralized foreign policy but that was not all; he was completely opposed to any centralized machinery of any kind. Even on such a routine question as that of compiling and publishing Empire trade statistics, Canadian nationalism clashed with British officialdom. The Board of Trade wanted to issue the statistics under the authority of an advisory committee made up of the High Commissioner. R. H. Coates, who represented Canada at this particular discussion, vetoed the proposal with the full approval and applause of Dafoe and Skelton. A proposal for an Imperial Economic Committee and a plan to put the Imperial Shipping Committee on a statutory basis were also dropped because of a Canadian fear that they might develop into some form of centralized machinery. The obvious satisfaction with which Dafoe recorded these events is, in part, explained by his dislike and distrust of Whitehall bureaucrats. At Paris in 1919 an officious civil servant tried to throw him out of a meeting because he did not represent a British paper; the official had been unable to place Canada in his mind. That evening Dafoe wrote in his diary: " ... is it any wonder with things like this happening that there are Canadians who think it is about time to cut the painter." In 1921 he wrote in an editorial: "There is not a permanent official in Whitehall who has any other conception of the Dominions than as dependent colonies subordinate in the last analysis to the British parliament ... every assertion of national equality for the Dominions is regarded as just so much idle patter having no actual relationship to the fact."

Another reason for Dafoe's inveterate hostility to any form of central machinery in the Empire of Commonwealth was a conviction, honestly held, that the strength of the group lay in a spontaneous moral unity which would be destroyed by centralization. This moral unity was based on a common heritage of British parliamentary institutions, dedication to such values as the rule of law, and allegiance to a common, symbolic, and divisible sovereign. This view of Commonwealth left no room for India and the African territories, and Dafoe was convinced in the 1920's that they should go their own way, but this anti-colonialism moderated as he grew older.

Dafoe's view of Commonwealth was, in many ways, typical of the liberal nationalist. He envisaged a loose, undefined, and amorphous Commonwealth as a political solution to an internal problem in Canada—as a political device to satisfy the ancestral attitudes of the loyalists and pacify all but the most extreme of the nationalists. He also displayed another attitude which has become typically Canadian, that of attempting to derive the maximum benefit from the Commonwealth association with the minimum investment. For example, at the Imperial Conference of 1923, the Canadian group vetoed the proposal to put the Imperial Shipping

Committee on a statutory basis, to pay its chairman, Sir Halford MacKinder, a salary, and to require each country to share this and other expenses. A year later the Canadian government complained of discrimination in ocean freight rates and requested an investigation by the Committee. Dafoe found the Committee slow to grasp the Canadian case, complained that it was ineffective, and concluded one editorial as follows: "Call you this a backing by your friends. ... The *Free Press* feels free to say that a little indignation over the discrimination would become the chairman of the Imperial Shipping Committee and would tend to strengthen the confidence of the people in the worth of that Committee."

There is a pattern, a line of development, in the thought and activity of J. W. Dafoe. As in many other self-made men there were elements of bigotry and intolerance in his earlier stands on public issues, but, unlike some, he never stopped growing, and during the last fifteen years of his life capped many of his early ideas with concepts of statesmanship. His views on Canadian unity, while always rooted in pride and hope, had sometimes been strident, intolerant, and unreasonable. This was particularly true of his suspicions of the Roman Catholic hierarchy and his manifest impatience with any defence of separate schools. He became unreasonable over the question of the Hudson's Bay Railway and repeatedly accused those who questioned its financial feasibility of being narrow-minded, greedy Easterners concerned only with extracting their pound of flesh from the West; Ottawa and Toronto newspapers were, he wrote, like Pavlov's dogs: mention the Hudson's Bay Railway and they began to bark and froth at the mouth. All this was put behind him when he became a member of the Rowell-Sirois Commission in 1937, and his unique knowledge of Canadian history was brought to bear in a statesmanlike way on national problems. When Duplessis was unspeakably rude, Dafoe turned the other cheek and asked one of his colleagues to reply politely in French. There had been occasions, particularly in the 1920's, when his nationalism hit a strident note, when he took a malicious delight in labelling those who questioned his assumptions as "colonially minded." But he capped this with a constructive and forceful advocacy of internationalism and collective security. Men like O. D. Skelton and Loring Christie, whose views were so close to his own in 1923, were left far behind in

112

their isolationism, an isolationism built mainly on ideas that Dafoe himself once shared.

Dafoe's defence of the League of Nations and of the principle of collective security made him an international figure. In 1941 he wrote:

September is a month of tragic anniversaries. Germany invaded Poland on September 1st, 1939, Great Britain declared war on Germany, September 3rd, Canada did likewise on September 10th. But there is a still more tragic anniversary. It was on September 18th, 1931—ten years ago today, that the Japanese army staged the Mukden incident ... on that day, in that remote place, a fuse was lighted that has blown to pieces the world order that was envisaged by the Covenant of the League of Nations.

He refrained from saying "I told you so," but he had done just that in an editorial entitled "Watchman, What of the Night" and written within a few months after the Japanese attack: "Nations must not be judges in their own quarrels ... the application of force to the settlement of disputes or to the furthering of national interests must be definitely and finally outlawed." He recalled and quoted many times the words he had heard Wilson speak in Paris in 1919: "Armed force is in the background and if the moral force of the world will not suffice to keep the peace the physical force of the world shall."

Between 1931 and 1939 he wrote nearly one thousand editorials in defence of the League and collective security, all based on his conviction that "the political world must be a single community and not a collection of irresponsible sovereign states. The change is the same as the change within a state when the rule of law replaced private vengeance in dealing with criminals. Under this theory Italy's need for colonies is as irrelevant as a burglar's need for a meal." Other relevant subjects were treated and given the usual massive documentation: the short-sightedness and stupidity of national leaders, the errors of the Versailles Peace Treaty, the continuance of traditional old-fashioned views of national interest, public apathy, pacifism, the mad dance of economic nationalism, intransigence, war debts, reparations, ill-treatment of minorities, cowardice, treachery, isolationism, the "little Canadian foreign office," Mackenzie King, Hoare, and Laval. When the League was unable to apply sanctions in 1936 and Dafoe began to predict

113

war, he wrote: "and down the road, not faraway in point of time, will be the world's greatest war, the hyperbolic war, the war that will never stop until the structure of society, as we know it, will sink into the slime." In 1937 he wrote:

Is imagination a lost faculty? If there are any who still have it let them exercise it by trying to translate the cold words which appear in the news dispatches from Shanghai into reality ... bombardment, panic, fires, stampedes, death by bombs, by mutilation, by falling walls of fire; homelessness, hunger ... just try to imagine a rain of bombs on London, Paris or Prague.

Dafoe wrote this way because he believed that the leadership in every country was wrong and that public opinion, an international public opinion, must be created to outlaw war by international organization. The newspaper had a role to fill and a mission to discharge—a responsibility more significant than want ads, comic strips, or even the provision of news. It must lead public opinion. But he did not stop with editorials. He became President of the Canadian Institute of International Affairs, a body he had helped found as a member of a group that met at Borden's house in Ottawa in 1928. He was Chairman of the Institute of Pacific Relations from 1936 to 1938. He addressed a very large number of public meetings, service clubs, graduating classes, and so on, and was heard on the radio. Sometimes he wondered if it was all worth it; he wrote Edward Carter in 1940:

The war came pretty near flattening me out. It gave me such a feeling of frustration—of saying what's the use. The damn world is hell bent on suicide. I thought of how so many friends of mine have been busy for 20 years saving the world: Carter, Shotwell, old Dr. Butler, Lord Cecil, League of Nations Societies, International Conciliation, the I.P.R., Chatham House, the Canadian Institute, etc., etc.... along come a couple of crazy men who fifty years ago would have been locked up as bums or worse and half the people of the world follow them as the Pied Piper into darkness, insanity and savagery. All our work seems to have gone for nothing. But perhaps not. It is with that hope that I guess we must carry on as best we can.... I still take the odd poke at barbarians with a sort of growing hope that perhaps my contribution, such as it is, is not wasted.

The last editorial he wrote, dated January 6, 1944, (he died on the ninth) was on Wilson, and ended: "Whatever mistakes Wilson may have made, they are dust in the balance in judging the greatness of his work and its enduring qualities."

J. W. Dafoe's whole adult life was devoted to newspapers; he began his career as a cub reporter and ended it over sixty years later as a great editor who ranks with other greats such as C. P. Scott, Thomas Barnes, Delane, William Allen White. When the *Free Press* celebrated its fiftieth birthday in 1922, Dafoe wrote an editorial giving his conception of what a newspaper ought to be. While he was well aware that newspapers can exist only if they are viable commercial enterprises and that freedom of the press owes its origin to the growth of advertising revenue, yet he believed with great and unshakable conviction that the relationship between the newspaper and the community was much more than a mere matter of business. Nor could the paper be satisfied with the role of recorder and narrator but must also be commentator, critic, a supporter of causes, a forum for debate, a meeting-place of minds and interests, and a vehicle for encouragement of the arts. As he put it in conclusion: "It is greater than any individual or combination of individuals, it has its own corporate life, its traditions, its memories, its policies, its standards—in short it has its own individuality, the sum of all the energies and labour which have been expended upon it by its directors, managers, editors, assistants and employees of all kinds."

Dafoe symbolized the independence and individuality of the paper. Because he was a great editor he could gather a highly competent and completely devoted staff around him—men like Grant Dexter, George Ferguson, J. B. McGeachy, and many others whose names are less familiar. He had an immense knowledge of his craft, a great loyalty to the journalistic trade, and a remarkable tolerance of the foibles of reporters. One story will illustrate. In the 1920's a Mr. Chisholm was a *Free Press* representative in Ottawa. Chisholm could, when sober, produce acceptable copy, but his judgment and discretion left much to be desired. In 1922 Sir Clifford Sifton gave an important address to the Ottawa Canadian Club, but his paper's representative was unable to cover it. The publisher was, understandably, irked; he wrote a long and strong letter on the need for efficiency, and closed by demanding Chisholm's dismissal. Dafoe refused. A few years later, Chisholm, bored with the drone of debate in the

Commons, left his place in the Press Gallery to enliven his spirits over a drink with some cronies. He missed an item of vital interest to Winnipeg and the rival paper got a scoop. In reply to a request for an explanation, Chisholm wired simply, "Weather here oppressively hot." This incident became one of Dafoe's favourite trade stories.

Some aspects of *Free Press* internal politics were, however, far from funny. E. H. Macklin, the business manager and publisher's representative, came to the paper a few months before Dafoe and in the early days occupied a dominant position. But Dafoe became the paper, and the manager's primacy was replaced by a consuming jealousy, a jealousy which found expression in innumerable petty actions, in intrigue against the editor within the office and at the Manitoba Club. When Dafoe began attacking Bennett the day after his election and the circulation of the paper fell, Macklin got support from one of the sons of Sir Clifford to replace the editor. Dafoe never mentioned this struggle to anyone, perhaps because he knew that when the chips were down he would win. In 1934 Macklin was forcibly retired and Dafoe was made President of the Company.

Dafoe's great personal integrity is reflected in his ability to keep a confidence, and, so far as is known, he never broke one. His success as an editor is, in part, due to the unrivalled sources of behind-the-scenes information he built up both in Ottawa and Washington, and his sources were by no means confined to close political friends. He also had a most remarkable memory; one of his rivals in the newspaper business and opponent politically has written: "There seemed to be no end to the quantity of information and quotations stored in his memory and no limit to his ability to call on what he wanted when he wanted it." Of course his memory was supplemented by the best newspaper library in Canada. This massive filing system and sponge-like memory was, in one sense, a disadvantage. Many of his editorials were turgid and over-documented. Despite the fact that he could write well he used the sledge-hammer and not the rapier; his technique was often like that of a pneumatic battering-ram. Yet this technique is partly explained by the exceptional strength of the man's convictions and his belief that the newspaper must shape as well as inform public opinion. He would have applauded the views of

Thomas Barnes, the original "thunderer" of the *Times*, who stated a century earlier: "John Bull, whose understanding is rather sluggish—and I speak of the majority of readers—requires a strong stimulus. He dozes composedly over his prejudices which his conceits call opinions and you must fire ten pounders at his densely compacted intellect before you can make it comprehend your meaning or care one farthing for your efforts."

Freedom of the press was close to Dafoe's heart, and he would not compromise this principle even if the pressure came from a pleading friend, an angry and powerful public figure, or, as rarely happened, the publishers. In 1938 George Ferguson, who was acting as editor in Dafoe's absence, got hold of and published a document on C.P.R. policy which had not been intended for publication. Edward Beatty, the Chairman of the Board, wrote a bitter letter, and Dafoe replied:

Between newspapers which publish news inconvenient to governments, corporations, interests, etc., and the parties thus inconvenienced there are often differences of opinion as to the propriety of these publications; but that the public interest is, as a general rule, better served by the newspaper being the sole judge in these matters, subject always of course to its responsibility to the law, is a view which I am prepared to defend.

In 1937 McGill University dismissed its principal and, when the *Free Press* carried an editorial asking for a public statement, the Chancellor wrote the editor assuring him that no question of academic freedom was involved and requesting no more publicity. Dafoe left the letter unanswered until he was able to verify the truth of the statement through his own independent investigation.

On the editorial page he was without mercy, but in personal relationships he was exceptionally magnanimous. Indeed he sometimes, but always secretly, befriended the person he had attacked politically. When the western Social Service Bureau, headed by J. S. Woodsworth, was abolished, Dafoe felt sure that the action had resulted from Woodsworth's pacificism. He protested, unsuccessfully, and then attempted to get him a chair at the University of Manitoba. He fired many editorial broadsides at John Queen, Winnipeg's socialist mayor, but when the battles were over he worked behind the scenes to get Queen appointed to a

117

government position because he suspected he was down and out. When Dafoe died in 1944, there were many testimonials in leading newspapers throughout the English-speaking world as to his integrity, character, and influence. The one that the family remembers best came from a humble labourer, the man who cut the inscription on the gravestone. He went to the house and said simply that years ago when he worked at the *Free Press* Dafoe had helped him over a rough spot in life, and he wanted the family to know that he appreciated it.

EMILY CARR

It is a great pleasure and a great honour to speak to you here, in this institution which has attained the status of a major Canadian university, in the capital city of our country, and under the auspices of the Institute of Canadian Studies which has already done much to bring into focus the Canadian tradition. And it is altogether fitting that this formal gesture of homage and this institutional recognition should be directed towards an old woman who had as little as possible to do with institutions or formalities of any kind during her lifetime. For this, surely, is in the habit and tradition of Canadian life, that the impulse of the individual soul, in its uniqueness, in its creativeness, should at last be made part of the national impulse, the collective tradition.

It is with the hope of furthering this transfusion of what Milton called "the lifeblood of a master spirit" into the stream of our national culture that I shall try to engage your attention this evening. Not that this paper is or can be definitive in any sense. We must look to someone like Ira Dilworth, the friend and literary executor of Emily Carr, for the final summing-up. All to whom Emily Carr and her work have significance owe him a debt of gratitude for his selfless, timely, and tactful service. May I here express my thanks to him as well as to Jack Shadbolt for their help in sharpening my image of her achievement.

The first thing that strikes one in considering the life and work of Emily Carr is the effect which her surroundings had upon her. The physical and social setting which the Pacific Coast provided were decisive influences in her life. It is useful to recall briefly what these were.

British Columbia, the province in which Emily Carr was born, where she lived, worked, and died, comes near to rivalling Australia in the lateness of its effective discovery and settlement. The sea voyage from Europe, either by Cape Horn or the Cape of Good Hope, was of immense length. Even the voyage from Spanish Pacific ports was long, dangerous, and unpromising. On the landward side a perfect sea of mountains backed by immense reaches of the prairie separated the West Coast from eastern Canadian and American settlement.

It is not surprising, therefore, to find both Russian and Spanish efforts at exploration and trade becoming attenuated as they reached what is now British Columbia. It is not surprising to find the last northwest thrust of American colonization terminating in the lower valley of the Columbia. It is less clearly understandable that, in spite of the large influx of settlers from Great Britain, British social and cultural influence has become steadily more diffuse as older generations have passed away and as their children and grandchildren have come under the influence of Canadian and West-Coast American ways. Even the charming city and district of Duncan, as time goes on, look less and less like a fragment of the south of England set down among the mountains of Vancouver Island. And to complete the pattern, it must be recognized that although British Columbia is a part of Canada it has been in many ways as remote and different from the rest of the country as California from the rest of the United States.

Emily Carr was born in 1871 in a Victoria which superficially had the air of a British community but which was at certain levels a temporary amalgam of unstable social elements. As a child she found herself in a partial vacuum in which some good-sized molecules of British civilization were circulating. That she did not experience in her childhood or even in her middle years the advantages of a mature culture and a homogeneous community is all too apparent in the pages of her memoir, *Growing Pains*. She made friends wherever she went, but she never found a congenial society of fellow artists or of those who had a wide understanding of the arts. She was very much alone.

As one who was also a child in Victoria, one full generation later, and who saw friends grow up there who were aspiring painters, I confess to feeling rather intimately Emily Carr's predicament, which was, by the recoil of her strong will and the intensity of her effort, a main source of her unique artistic achievement. Her difficulty was in not having points of reference. Lawren Harris, in his introduction to the catalogue of her paintings and drawings, has some perceptive remarks on this subject:

The good people of her native city were decidedly Victorian in outlook and quite naturally so. They considered art as a minor and ladylike social grace, not as a social force. They had imported their way of life and seeing from the old land and being further removed and more isolated from the rest of Canada than any other sizeable community, there was almost nothing in art to stir them and change their outlook. Moreover the equable and lovely climate of Victoria made it easy and pleasant to maintain their conservative way of life. A powerful creative individual in their midst such as Emily Carr was an anomaly.

Victoria, as a repository of British social and cultural values, wears a face whose lineaments are capable of various interpretations. Perhaps you will pardon some unscholarly *obiter dicta* from one who as a child lived within a few blocks of where Emily Carr was born and attended a school the playground of which lay within the Beacon Hill Park so familiar to readers of her autobiographical books.

The mind of a child could find little to fasten on firmly. The history of the West Coast was of short duration and afforded few heroes or dramatic events. Cook, Fraser, Thompson, Douglas: none of them could well have an appeal comparable to the carefully realized archetypes that arise at the mention of King Alfred, Drake, Cromwell, Wellington, or Nelson. Victoria has never, since its foundation, changed hands between great powers or seen an insurrection or invasion. There is little memory of crisis.

In New Zealand English settlers produced a Canterbury, and Scots a Dunedin, but in Victoria tens of thousands of English and Scots, not forgetting Irish and Welsh, came in and found neither a centre of attraction about which their energies could be brought into play nor an external pressure against which they were obliged to combine. Institutions likely to act as centripetal forces had a

121

way of dissolving. The Crown colony of Vancouver Island disappeared in 1866. In 1905 Esquimault ceased to be a Royal Navy base. The system of private schools, founded on English models, never achieved an adequate financial basis. Admirable and long-sustained efforts by individuals were not enough.

Nor could Victoria's position as capital of the province quite provide the magnetism needed to satisfy the imagination. The account given in Margaret Ormsby's history of the province of disreputable politics, land-grabbing, and partisan tactics repels the idealizing mind. And this is in some way related to the inexplicable fact that, while British and American historians have contrived to extract what look like symbols of heroism and aspiration from even the least reputable parts of the national history, Canadian historians have been too straightforward to do so.

Oddly enough, it has been the two wars that have stimulated pride, devotion, and conscious cohesion in the community of Victoria. The service of Victorians in two world wars is a matter of great and just pride. But these events were too late to affect the growing sensibility of Emily Carr, whose generation was becoming too old for service when the first war broke out.

I should perhaps make it explicit that these remarks apply to old Victoria and not to the contemporary city and society, with its strong cultural interests and its thriving university. I should also admit the strongly subjective bias of these judgments, which you may, however, be willing to tolerate because they seek to throw light on the childhood of Emily Carr, a highly subjective person.

If old Victoria did not supply her with a frame of reference or a society of kindred souls, it did something else which in the long run was decisive in her development. Abundant and overwhelming natural beauty was at her door. The partially tamed wildness of Beacon Hill Park, the rocky foreshore with its many bays, the wide strait of Juan de Fuca, the changing symmetry of the Cascade Mountains beyond. On the other side, the purple silhouette of the Sooke Hills, the inland salt waters of the Gorge, the two rocky and tree-clad heights of Mount Tolmie and Cedar Hill. And everywhere, easily accessible from Emily Carr's Victoria, the stands of virgin forest, fir and cedar and hemlock, which finally claimed her eye and heart and imagination.

Of her life we know a great deal. The autobiographical books are filled with detail. But because she disliked self-analysis in writing submitted for publication, we are not always drawn below the surface of her story. We must dig down a bit for the implications.

Without doubt her relations with her family were ambivalent. For her mother, who died when she was twelve, she felt deep affection and affinity. For her father, who lived till she was fourteen, there was warm affection mingled with some distaste for his disposition of the family routine. For her eldest sister she felt an active dislike. Resentment of her sister's friends and her sister's discipline reached a peak of fury when she was nearly sixteen. She would escape into the country on an old pony, into what she later described as "the deep lovely places that were the very foundation on which my work as a painter was to be built."

At all times her relations with people in general strike the present-day reader as odd. The proportion of unpleasant individuals she encountered appears unreal, and one is inclined to put her down as touchy, supersensitive, over-critical. Such was my own feeling on recently rereading *The House of All Sorts* where her woes as owner and keeper of an apartment-house are detailed. But suddenly came the shock of recognition. It happened that I used to own a very small house in Victoria, of a kind that attracted as tenants the same class as came to Emily to rent her apartments. For several years I had tenants who were probably the lineal descendants of her tenants. I absolve her of all uncharitableness. I only marvel that she did not resort to violence.

This leads one to pause and wonder whether Emily's hatred of London and of so much in English life might not be equally explicable. Her reaction to the six other paying guests in her first London *pension* is direct and simple: "I hated them right away." Of London itself she says simply: "I hate it." She makes a few friends but she never feels friendly towards English society. "I don't like your English ways," is her verdict. Of her expeditions about London she records, "We were always doing things that were right for Canada but found they were wrong in England. ... I hate, hate, hate, London." Let us try to put ourselves in her place. She came to England as a young woman without a grain of class ambition, without tact, without decent social hypocrisy, without knowledge of the world and utterly without *savoir faire. Pouvoir faire* was all she understood, and she got on with her work. It was the late Victorian and Edwardian world that she encountered (she stood at the back of a crowd to see the funeral procession of the old Queen) and there can have been few other periods in English history when meaningless snobbery and petty class distinction flourished in such style. The purgation of two wars and a vast social upheaval was still in the future. She liked St. Paul's, she loved Kew Gardens, but she loathed the British Museum, she hated aspidistras and she was sickened by slums. She could not endure the English obsession with history. Only when at times she could reach the timeless beauty of the English countryside was she happy. At St. Ives she forsook the glare of sunlight on the beach and took her sketching materials to Tregenna Wood where she records, "ivy crept up the tree trunks to hang down in curtains." A big white sow came by every day at lunch-time to share her sandwiches. (If these were of pork, then out of delicacy Emily offered her friend only the crust.)

This is perhaps the place, if at all, to consider why Emily Carr never married. She had repeated opportunities and, at least once, before she went to England, she fell in love. One can only conjecture that her great capacity for devotion early turned from the frustrations of her family and social environment and made its own channel into the world of nature. Her love for flowers and trees, for animals and poor Indians, was a deep current cutting its way through all the entanglements of her existence.

Emily's adult life was filled with annoyances and frustrations. She came back from France in 1911 and did little but struggle to live until Marius Barbeau, hearing of her in the Indian villages, in his kindness sought her out and made it possible for her to visit and exhibit in the East. For fifteen years, while keeping her apartment-house, she had no leisure or strength to paint. But the current of her vitality only went underground. She never really deviated from her goal, which was to express fully in painting her transcendent sense of life. Success came to her slowly and only after immense bafflement from persons and circumstances, but she outgrew and outlasted them all. Her sign manual, so to speak, in her sketches and paintings, is a small spirillic tree, and one likes to think that this is in some sense symbolic of her own life. Where low-lying land has been intermittently cleared or burned over,

124

one sees here and there, among the deciduous trees that spring up
at once, a small evergreen which, although hardly noticeable, will
in the long run triumph and become a giant. It is a sight to stir the
imagination, and I have tried to express its relation to the subject
of this paper in a sonnet, which although it is a very simple verse
you will perhaps permit me to read to you.

> A young cedar, lost among the alders.
> Look where she clambers in an eager spiral
> Of feathery frond, a spire to sun aspiring,
> While underfoot the black leaves slip in water.
> Crows flap over. The slow season alters.
> Winter's sun in a dull fog half hiding
> Shows the alders, black trunks strongly striding
> To hem her in. Her little greenness halts.
> But come once more! Come when fifty years
> Have frosted you. Come in summer and see
> Her rising high to fill the welcoming skies.
> The last black stick rots down and disappears,
> But her enormous billow wild and free
> Flings into sunlight where the eagle flies.

Emily Carr's writing is without question marginal to her painting, and yet it is work of great interest and much more an artistic
creation in its own right than the initial impression it gives of
simple style and subject-matter would suggest. Her books form an
autobiographical continuum with some overlapping, and they may
properly be regarded as a single work. *Klee Wyck*, published in
1941, is a set of impressions of the Indians and the Indian villages
she had encountered in her sketching trips up the coast. *The Book
of Small*, which appeared in 1942, told of her childhood in Victoria.
As the youngest girl of the family, she was appropriately "Small."
Growing Pains, which passes quickly over the period dealt with
in detail by *The Book of Small,* carries her autobiography to
within three or four years of her death, and appeared in 1946.
The House of All Sorts, which came out in 1944, details her
struggles to make a living by renting apartments, breeding dogs,
making pottery. There are unpublished journals and letters in
the custody of Ira Dilworth, her literary executor, which will in
due course be published to complete the story.

The apparant naïveté of Emily Carr's style and apparent simplicity of much of her subject-matter do not conceal from the responsive reader that he has in his hands a piece of chronicle of which every page compels him to turn to the next and which is in sum a valuable contribution to the spiritual history of its time and place. The pervasive note of all her writing is an extreme sensitiveness to direct impressions. She is no sensualist, nor even particularly sensuous, but the encounters with life which the daily round and the constant pursuit of perfection bring fill her with delight, with awe, with sorrow, with disgust, with rage. And in her chosen retreat of the deep woods she experiences a life of nature resembling her own deepest strivings. This life it becomes her passion to experience, to understand, to record, to interpret. There was a great reciprocal flow of power between her soul and the spirit of the woods which makes of her later paintings and sketches a series of statements in which the objective and subjective elements are perfectly and permanently fused.

A brief passage from her sketch entitled "Skedans" (*Klee Wyck*) will illustrate how direct sense impressions by gradations of subjective addition become a path toward identification of writer and scene:

To the right of Skedans were twin cones of earth and rock. They were covered to the top with trees and scrub. The land ran out beyond these mounds and met the jagged reefs of the bay.

We broke through growth above our heads to reach the house. It was of the old type, but had been repaired a little by halibut fishers who still used it occasionally. The walls were full of cracks and knot-holes. There were stones, blackened by fire, lying on the earth floor. Above them was a great smoke-hole in the roof; it had a flap that could be adjusted to the wind. Sleeping-benches ran along the wall and there was a rude table made of driftwood by the halibut fishers. (Indians use the floor for their tables and seats.)

When the fire roared, our blankets were spread on the platforms and Louisa's stew-pot simmered. The place was grand—we had got close down to real things. In Skedans there were no shams.

When night came we cuddled into our blankets. The night was still. Just the waves splashed slow and even along the beach. If your face was towards the wall, the sea tang seeped in at the cracks and poured over it; if you turned round and faced in, there was the lovely smoky smell of our wood fire on the clay floor.

Early in the morning Jimmie stirred the embers; then he went out

126

and brought us icy water from the spring to wash our faces in. He cut
a little path like a green tunnel from the house to the beach, so that
we could come and go easily. I went out to sketch the poles.

They were in a long straggling row the entire length of the bay and
pointed this way and that; but no matter how drunken their tilt, the
Haida poles never lost their dignity. They looked sadder, perhaps,
when they bowed forward and more stern when they tipped back. They
were bleached to a pinkish silver colour and cracked by the sun, but
nothing could make them mean or poor, because the Indians had put
strong thought into them and had believed sincerely in what they were
trying to express.

The twisted trees and high tossed drift-wood hinted that Skedans
could be as thoroughly fierce as she was calm. She was downright
about everything.

If at one pole of her being Emily Carr repelled and was repelled
by a whole series of inimical and unsympathetic people and things,
she was, as I have said, equally and simultaneously attracted to a
few friends, to animals and birds, to Indians in their villages, and
to the trees of the forest. And her feelings flow into words of the
most direct and immediate kind. She had none of the masks of
the artist; she was always simply, unmistakably, consistently, in
her life and her work, herself. To meet her was to experience impact, and her pictures often have the same effect. Leaving St.
Joseph's Hospital in Victoria one evening, hurrying along a
twilight passage hung with conventional religious pictures, I felt
something on the wall strike my eye. It was a small painting of
wild lilies (the Easter lily or dog-tooth violet) done by Emily Carr
and given to the hospital in gratitude for the nursing of her sister.

The reason she liked Indians was not that they were noble
savages or bearers of the primitive virtues. She liked them because
they were themselves. At the conclusion of a brief sketch of Jenny-
Two-Bits, an old Indian woman who asked twenty-five cents for
whatever she had to sell, we see Jenny and her old blind husband
beachcombing or fishing together, in utter poverty. The last sentence reads, "When they caught a fish or when Jenny sold something for two bits or when they sat together baking themselves in
the sunshine, they were happy enough." This is neither Classicism,
nor Romanticism, nor Naturalism: just Emily Carr sensing and
expressing in the most simple and direct way how two old Indian

127

nobodies take life from day to day. Let us not make extravagant claims for this kind of writing. But let us see that it has honesty, freshness, and durability. Indeed it possesses these qualities in a kind of absolute form which will probably make her a classic of Canadian literature as long as Canadian literature shall be read or remembered.

For animals she had an instinctive and immediate affinity. Her pages are full of them, from the song-birds she nurtured in England hoping to send them to Canada, to the bobtailed sheep-dogs she bred for many years to make a living. Everyone will have his own choice of her innumerable animal stories. Mine is that of the dogs at the deserted village of Greenville, abandoned and starving. She did what she could for them and one of them finally let her pull porcupine quills out of its face. "It was people they wanted," she says, "even more than food." As she left, she tells us, "The dogs followed to the edge of the water, their stomachs and hearts sore at seeing us go. Perhaps in a way dogs are more domestic and more responsive than Indians." Animals got a lion's share of her affection throughout her life.

Her feelings toward trees are all of a piece with her feelings toward Indians or animals but, unlike the latter, they are inextricable from the substance of her painting and can only be considered in that context. She achieved a passionate and instinctive identity of feeling with the forest which is unique in Canadian painting. It is too sweeping a generalization to say that only her forest pictures have any value, but if with the forest pictures we put the pictures of totem poles—which are trees from whose substance the carver's axe and chisel have released the inward tutelary power of the forest landscape—we shall find that they constitute the substance if not quite the sum of her achievement.

Her paintings may be regarded in several ways. We may see them as a revelation of the forms and atmosphere of the forest. We may see them as the history of a technique which was slowly developed as she passed from youthful experiments, to an American art school, to an English school and to instruction in France, and finally back to the environs of Victoria where she could work out her problems face to face with the landscape itself. Or we may think of her work as autobiography, an attempt to record with

128

evergrowing freedom and effectiveness—although in the face of great overwhelmings of spirit—the life force which beat with equal pulse in her and in the green current of the foliage.

It is the last consideration that must ultimately triumph. Every aspect of her work finally turns into this autobiographical statement, this testimony to her integrity. She was unique among Canadian painters of her time, I think, in pursuing with such singleness the search for something in the landscape that would respond and correspond to her own spirit. Phrases like "life force" and "identity with nature" are old-fashioned now, but how else are we to express the object of her quest? For a quest for ultimate solutions it was, as her books reveal.

She was not primarily interpreting Canada to the world. She was interpreting herself to herself by the symbols which the forest provided. At one pole of her experience was her own subjective longing and striving, and at the other was the objective fact of the great forest forms in their light and shade. In the field of force set up by this polarity she sat and painted, and the brush strokes of her later years have the same air of being compelled as the lines of filings on paper do in a similar situation.

What she produces is not primarily an image of complexity or of secret absorption. She has rather seized the immemorial and atavistic image of the jungle, the maze, the Gothic wood with its promise of endless revelation of strange forces. But she does not, cannot, need not render the whole of this great complex. She instinctively intensifies the image of force, of energy surging or thrusting up into a burst of life and always with reserves latent and unexpended. One of the favourite forms of her middle period is the spiral or vortex. There is almost certainly no direct connection between these preoccupations of hers and the thrusts of energy and vortex movements in Baroque painting, but it would be curious to try to discover whether some deep affinity did not exist.

How far we can employ Freudian symbolism in the same context I do not know and have not the skill to find out. But I should like to quote as an example of perception and tact a sentence or two written by one of her friends:

I dont want to utter a sacrilege nor suggest any phony psychoanalytical analysis, but I can't escape a certain suggestion of the Freudian unconscious obsessions in those deep forest canvases which are generally so womb-like and phallic. I hasten to add that this is merely an observation as to the nature of their forms and has no bearing on their artistic achievement. Also I am aware how crude this kind of observation seems in a Canadian context—and to those who knew Emily Carr, how offensive this must seem to her so pure, incandescent spirit. Yet I see no harm in the observation.

Her actual technical progression was one continuous struggle. Her sketches supplement her canvases in showing how she slowly abandoned representational and somewhat picturesque scenes for trees and poles and rocks reduced to a kind of solid geometry. Here the influence of Lawren Harris and of the forms he had derived from cubism is almost certainly visible. This was a necessary stage before she could reach her own variety of abstraction. In her struggle to free her own inner energies, she had to pass through various technical experiments of which the effort to reduce form to geometrical essentials was only one. She tested shape against shape. Her columnar or pyramidal trees with their sometimes heavily terraced foliage or their blankets of green which surge or spiral upwards—these were not easily amenable forms, or forms for whose juxtaposition there was some conventional solution. In general, European painters had not chosen to immerse themselves in coniferous forest. And her heavy, struggling shapes, moving deeper into the forest, had to be reconciled with the insistent demands of the picture plane. The problems of perspective she largely avoided.

She had also some difficulties with her medium of a practical kind having to do with the raw materials of her craft. She did a good many rapid sketches in oils and used gasoline as a thinner. Many of her larger paintings have poor surfaces. This may have some relation to her poverty, but it seems more likely that she worked so far from the centres and traditional homes of painting that she felt little incentive to send away for proper materials.

Her self-absorption may also be held accountable for the strong infusion of literary sentimentalism in her earlier work. She took some time to get over painting for effect and producing subject pictures. Not that some of these fail to achieve striking success, such as "Blunden Harbour" here in the National Gallery. It is somewhat theatrical, but it comes off unmistakably.

Through all these problems, however, she made her way toward her final liberation. She broke the barrier. She liberated herself and her art, and who would quarrel with the means that she employed? She established a dominion over certain themes, forms, and colours which made them her servants and obliged them to carry the insignia of her private and passionate experience: the forest cavern, the heaving heavily fleeced cedar, certain tones of green and grey.

Her mood, it has been well said, is like a Sibelius tone-poem—a fixation on grandeur, which she later transcended by forgetting it, passing naturally beyond it. Upon her little evergreen tree she played many variations. It became an abstraction to express a surge of cosmic life and finally to burn in an incandescent rhapsody. Hers was progress toward apotheosis, and this has nowhere received better expression than in Wilfred Watson's poem "Emily Carr":

> Like Jonah in the green belly of the whale
> Overwhelmed by Leviathan's lights and liver
> Imprisoned and appalled by the belly's wall
> Yet inscribing and scoring the uprush
> Sink vault and arch of that monstrous cathedral,
> Its living bone and its green pulsing flesh—
> Old woman, of your three days anatomy
> Leviathan sickened and spewed you forth
> In a great vomit on coasts of eternity.
> Then, as for John of Patmos, the river of life
> Burned for you an emerald and jasper smoke
> And down the valley you looked and saw
> All wilderness become transparent vapour,
> A ghostly underneath a fleshly stroke,
> And every bush an apocalypse of leaf.

What did she finally accomplish? Well, she was in a very real sense a pioneer and the daughter of a pioneer. Her love of personal freedom, her idiosyncrasy, her disregard of convention, her affinity for the forest, the beach, the Indian villages, all testify to the fact. In a society that looked uncertainly in more than one direction, she remained completely, unmistakably, consciously, creatively, and superbly herself. It was a considerable achievement. It is more than you or I will do.

She has helped to create an image of Canada in the Canadian

mind, and while this has been achieved by the use of two media, the subject-matter in neither case seeming to have much relation to the formal culture of this country, the effect is one of simple unity. Her life, her books, her canvases, all say the same thing and say it with overwhelming conviction—that in this world of stupidity and squalor the white fires of candour and courage still burn, that they illuminate the ill-defined but powerful ultimate truths of life. And these, most easily found in the gestures of simple people or in the face of nature itself, are the immemorial impulses of the will to live and to create, the impulse of charity towards life and hatred of all that impedes life.

She suffered deprivation: lack of a firm stratum of society, lack of sympathy, lack of a clientele, lack of constructive criticism, lack of money, lack of time, lack of good health and good luck, till all too near the end of her career. Her example proclaims itself with immense power. Like her, we can resist, work, escape, learn, endure, return, create, record, develop, and finally triumph.

It remains to assess the philistinism by which she felt herself largely surrounded. It was seldom vicious; there may have been a little derision, but there was a thousand times more involuntary neglect and disregard. Also, I am identifiably one of the Philistines who failed to appreciate her. About twenty years ago, sometime during the war years, Shadbolt took me to see her in her little house over James Bay. There were racks with rows of her sketches and paintings. They could have been bought for as little as twenty-five dollars apiece. Twenty-five dollars or even twice that sum could have been found. But it would have been necessary to transport these rather fragile things back to Winnipeg, and there was no proper place to hang them when one was in rooms. And it did not seem worth the effort, what with the struggle to live and make a living in a Winnipeg winter at that time. At bottom there was the unrecognized assumption that the visual arts do not really matter very much, so firmly rooted in the minds of those of us to whom making a living and achieving some kind of security has been a preoccupation. Pictures are nice but not necessary. We grow accustomed to dealing with reproductions and achieve no sense of the immediacy of artists and their work.

In a certain sense her life was a triumph. In another sense it was tragic. What might she not have accomplished if she had had

132

earlier and better instruction, the companionship of kindred spirits, the advice and assistance and affection of friends like Harris and especially Dilworth, twenty years earlier! In a country like Italy one sculptor or painter learns from another, every artist builds on the plastic and graphic inheritance from the past, a torso by Michelangelo is the lineal descendant of ancient Greek marbles, and nothing is born but out of the matrix of the common culture. How little of this Emily Carr experienced, and how little of what she experienced seems to have been mediated to her needs in a fruitful manner! These things are difficult to explain or judge, and in any case what different circumstances would have done for her is beyond our knowledge, though not beyond our conjecture. But there was waste, surely, very sad waste in her struggle to live and move and have her being as a creative artist.

Much as it may go against accepted methods of criticism I think the only sensible and sound way to judge Emily Carr is to have the facts of her life, the pages of her writings, and her drawings and paintings all in mind at the same time so that one may throw light on the other. She was a greater painter than writer, and a greater person than painter, and a greater soul than *persona*.

Her paintings, if I may briefly recapitulate, may be divided into half a dozen or more chronological groups. Those specially interested in this question of the ordering of her work may like to consult Paul Duval's "Emily Carr's was a Growing Art" (*Saturday Night*, 61 : 4-5) and R. S. Lambert's "Artistic Motives, Hidden and Revealed" (*Saturday Night*, 58 : 20).

There are paintings she did as an art-school student while she was in process of finding herself and her proper subject. There are those such as "The French Knitter" which belong to her period in France and show her drawn out of herself by the immense centripetal power of French practice. This influence persists for a short time after her return, when some of her impressionist skies exhibit, as Duval says, "forms soft and luminous, foliage gently rounded, sensitive texture, muted tones, pastel hues." She soon comes back to totem themes and to her own sterner and more limited palette. But she has moved forward; she has no longer the need to indulge in representation. But as she struggles to abstract the nature of visible forms, to set somewhat geometric results against one another, to balance space against space and to cope simultaneously with the demands of the picture plane and the desire for weight, depth, and movement, she comes to the point—it is fairly certain, though she dated very few of her paintings after she came back from France and disliked discussing their chronology—she comes to the point where the totems which she has always recognized as trees, both in her prose and in her paintings such as "Totem Forest," totems which have under the touch of Indian hands spoken their "strong talk," are no longer necessary. She is her own totem-maker now, and the trees, carved out by her brush, will speak their own tremendous secrets. As columns provide the Baroque architect with a means of expressing the thrust of human will which rises and identifies itself with divine will, so her tree trunks express her own upward thrust of energy and the energy of natural life rising from the inorganic rocks. And frequently these rising forms are partially or wholly draped by foliage abstracted into shapes as identifiably hers as the great draperies of El Greco are his. Sometimes this coniferous foliage, this enormous mass of greenness hangs like a valance or curls like a rising wave; but sometimes and most characteristically it is as though one had taken a strip of celestial sponge-rubber and wound it loosely and bulkily many times round the trunk, so that it forms a rough cone and its visible edge extends in an irregular and variable spiral ramp up toward the light. It is flesh, and the trunks of the trees are bones; we are inside the body of the forest.

And then she breaks out. As Lambert has well put it, she has passed through the dark forest and has emerged into the open under the skies, and the effect of a vortex of air slightly stirred by the seed of life within the matrix of the woods is released into dance-like rhythms across skies where the sun and wind create great spaces.

And this, I think, is all, though I am sure we have not released or developed all its meanings. She is an old woman who after a lifetime of struggle and long confinement has escaped into the harmonious spaces, the luminous home of clouds, the tree-tops rising into light, which are at the same moment the world of the rain forest on our Pacific margin and the world of her own liberated spirit.

134

HENRI BOURASSA

The reasons which have led me to make this study are mainly personal ones. I must, however, allude to them in order to justify the present undertaking and to indicate its scope.

I belong to a nationalistic *milieu*. Bourassa was part and parcel of my childhood: not that I knew him personally at the time, but I had been told his story, and his struggles seemed to me like the struggles of a paladin. He had been knighted by God Almighty to defend French Canadians against the injustices of Great Britain and of the various Canadian governments. Often vanquished, but always proud, always noble, always alert, his feats as a speaker began to look like veritable military campaigns. He had remained for French Canadians—and often in spite of opportunists of his own race, such as Laurier—the living rampart, the spotless and exacting hero fully dedicated to his one task. I often dreamt of this when I was a child.

Later I learned that the man I heard people speak of in these terms, the very man who was a legendary figure in the minds of boys of my age, that man was still alive. He edited a newspaper called *Le Devoir*. In 1925 he re-entered federal politics and was re-elected as the member for Labelle. At that time, like all youths of my age, I was only beginning to awaken to the political issues of the hour. Suddenly we became young men, and neither Bourassa nor many of the nationalists of the heyday of nationalism resembled the mental image we had formed of them.

Amongst these, Bourassa at least differed from the image in one important way. He proclaimed to us a nationalism that was Canadian first and foremost. He seemed to attack French-Canadian nationalism and its new representatives more willingly than he did the traditional British adversary. This became increasingly evident as the years went by. The Great Depression came, and the French Canadians were compelled to do some thinking. For them, radicalism found expression not in socialism but in a rather fierce nationalism mixed with strong demands for social and economic reform. And who became one of its most formidable adversaries? None other than Henri Bourassa.

Had we not been told the truth about him? It was said that Bourassa had had a change of heart, and a variety of reasons were given for this: a bad case of scruples, a severe reprimand from the Pope in 1926, political isolation, perhaps just a taste for contradiction. We therefore began to see the life of Bourassa as divided into two parts. There was the life of the fascinating hero who had begun a movement which we were to continue after him; and there was the life of the man who had returned from Rome completely changed, lost to us, who spoke only of religious duty and Canadian patriotism, and who set out boldly to cut down the harvest he had sown.

Such images do not satisfy the mind for long; in the end I found them too simple. Had Bourassa's disciples described his thought accurately? Did Bourassa contradict himself in this way? Had we not perhaps made the mistake of confusing the thought of Bourassa with that of Canon Lionel Groulx? In sum, what form of nationalism did Bourassa advocate throughout his life?

About nine years ago, circumstances compelled me to examine more closely the texts bequeathed to us by the founder of *Le Devoir*. My doubts were confirmed. Since then, I have carried this research further, and later this evening I shall give you the conclusions I have reached in the matter. In the meantime I want to discuss not Bourassa's life-work as a whole but his attitude toward his own race and toward our country. Because of his influence and the great value of his work, such a study should, I feel, interest not only French Canadians but all Canadians.

A word about Bourassa's life. He was the son of an artist, Napoléon Bourassa, and of the youngest daughter of Louis-Joseph

136

Papineau—the famous Papineau, the leader of the *patriotes*, the man of 1837. Born in 1868 in the very heart of Montreal, Bourassa lived there for some time. His education was sound enough, though somewhat irregular; he did not even get as far as his bachelor's degree. A sick man at the age of twenty, he moved to Montebello, where his grandfather had been *seigneur,* and there examined its every nook and cranny and became acquainted with its inhabitants. He won their love and respect. At the age of twenty-one he was elected mayor, and he was soon taking an active part in federal politics. In 1896 Laurier asked him to seek election in Labelle. He won the seat, and won it under the most auspicious circumstances: his leader, who had just assumed power, wished to groom him for more important functions.

But Bourassa was no slavish partisan, and as early as 1899 he had parted company with Laurier because of Canadian participation in the Boer War. He opposed Laurier's decision to send a Canadian expeditionary force to South Africa. He then resigned and explained his action in what proved to be a very important letter, for it marked the beginning of the anti-imperialist campaign he was to follow right up to 1944. He objected to the automatic participation of Canada in imperial wars. Let me quote the essential paragraphs of this letter:

Le principe en jeu est l'axiome par excellence du libéralisme anglais, c'est la base même du régime parlementaire: *No taxation without representation.* Et l'impôt du sang constitue la forme la plus lourde des contributions publiques.

Il s'agit de savoir si le Canada est prêt à renoncer à ses prérogatives de colonie constitutionelle, à sa liberté parlementaire, au pacte conclu avec la métropole après soixante-quinze ans de luttes—et à retourner à l'état primitif de colonie de la Couronne.

Il s'agit de décider si le peuple canadien sera appelé à prendre part à toutes les guerres de l'Empire sans que les portes du cabinet et du parlement impériaux lui soient ouvertes, sans même que ses représentants et son gouvernement soient consultés sur l'opportunité de ces luttes sanglantes.

Je ne consentirai jamais à appuyer cette politique rétrograde.

Citoyen britannique, fier de ses droits et jaloux de sa liberté, loyal à l'Angleterre et à son auguste souveraine, je suis prêt à payer de ma personne et de mes deniers, de ma parole et de mes actes, pour dé-

197

fendre le drapeau britannique dans toute l'étendue de la confédération canadienne.

Mais loyal avant tout, par-dessus tout et toujours au Canada, j'ai promis aux électeurs de mon comté de travailler au progrès de mon pays sans déroger à l'esprit fondamental de sa constitution. Pour accomplir cette promesse, j'ai donné mon appui à votre gouvernement tant que vous êtes resté dans les limites que le peuple canadien vous a tracées. J'ai approuvé et j'approuve encore votre politique administrative. Mais je vois dans ce dernier acte l'inauguration d'une politique constitutionelle que la majorité de vos partisans a toujours dénoncée et sur laquelle vous n'avez jamais consulté ni le Parlement ni l'électorat.

What Bourassa demanded and was to demand throughout his whole life, even if he did not demand formal independence through fear of the nearby American colossus, was an authentic autonomy of action for our country, a liberty of choice for Canadians who are, first and foremost, Canadians.

Laurier was wise enough to allow his "young and adamant friend" to be re-elected by acclamation. Bourassa came back as a federal member in 1900, and again in 1904, and it was at this point, with Olivar Asselin and several followers, that he founded the "Ligue nationaliste." He took part in all the debates in favour of schools for the minorities. Then he turned to provincial politics and was elected in 1907 in the counties of St. James and St. Hyacinthe. It was during this period that he launched several campaigns—notably, one against trusts—which were later to mark the beginning of more permanent movements. Provincial politics, however, proved unable to hold him for long. Frequent trips to Europe kept him abreast of international developments and convinced him that the situation was deteriorating. He therefore returned to the federal field.

Bourassa now had a powerful weapon for combat: *Le Devoir*, a daily newspaper which he founded in 1910 and around which he gathered a team of brilliant men. He was entering the best years of his life. In January he delivered in Notre Dame Church, during a Eucharistic Congress, a famous speech in which practically every French Canadian of the day could recognize himself. Elsewhere he increased his efforts against imperialism, though this did not hinder him from eulogizing Edward VII as the "serviteur vigilant et dévoué de ses peuples," or from inviting French Canadians to support vigorously the proposal to endow Montreal with a statue of the late king. But Bourassa opposed Laurier's naval policy, because he saw it as one more gesture that might drag Canada, should conditions prove favourable, into the wars of Great Britain.

In 1910, in the by-election for Drummond-Arthabaska, his candidate defeated Laurier's. Bourassa was unleashed; it was the moment of his greatest power. He was not a cabinet minister, nor a party leader, nor even a member of parliament; yet his influence alone, against Laurier, sufficed during the general elections of 1911 to elect twenty-seven Conservatives or Independents. Defeated in nearly every province, Laurier handed over the government to Borden. The prestige of the nationalist leader was greatly increased; in Quebec, while many blamed him, others praised him for Laurier's defeat.

War broke out. Bourassa, as it happened, had just returned from Europe. He hesitated briefly, and then, much against his better judgment, he accepted the principle of participation— which, however, he wanted to keep moderate. To rabid loyalists, such moderation looked like treason. An Ontario newspaper demanded Bourassa's arrest. The Canadian Club wanted to expel him but discovered the nationalist leader was not one of their members. Bourassa wrote them a letter which concluded as follows: "Plus j'avance dans la vie et plus je voyage dans le monde, plus se confirme ma conviction que je suis décidément pas trop britannique pour un milieu prussien comme le vôtre." This was a reference to another of Bourassa's undertakings: the increasingly frantic campaign in favour of French-Canadian residents of Ontario and against By-Law XVII, which in effect banished French from Ontario schools.

Then came conscription and the Union Cabinet. Laurier, doubtless in order to avoid leaving Quebec to Bourassa, refused to join it—a stand which earned him a complete victory in Quebec but a defeat in all the other provinces. Bourassa fought conscription violently before it was voted on; when it became law, he astonished everyone by his restraint and moderation.

The war over, Bourassa remained a fascinating figure. He played an important role in Ottawa as a member of parliament from 1925 to 1935, where he gave his opinion (and it was an opinion that carried considerable weight) on all major issues. But he was no longer the embodiment of the spirit of his people. It was at this time that he broke with the French-Canadian nationalists and began to denounce "leurs excès"—and I shall have more to say about this later. Having left *Le Devoir* in 1932, he lived in relative retirement, separated from the nationalists, his natural allies, until he joined them again in 1942, at the age of seventy-four, to fight Mackenzie King over the conscription issue and to support the *Bloc Populaire*. It was then only that I knew him personally. He died in 1952, more or less forgotten by the younger generation; yet his name remained the object of universal admiration. I might add that Professor Michael Oliver, who has studied the work of Bourassa rather closely, considers this aristocrat the precursor, in some respects, of a French-Canadian leftist movement.

With these preliminaries before us, we are now ready to broach the true subject of our inquiry: Bourassa's thought concerning the race and country to which he belonged.

The first time that Bourassa dealt at any length with the problems related to what he was later to call nationalism was, rather indirectly, during a campaign against imperialism. This is significant enough. The year was 1901. As a young member of parliament (he was only thirty-three) he was asked to define rigorously imperialism and its counterpart. He did so, on October 20, in a speech given at the *Théâtre National français* in which he said that the imperialism of the hour was "la contribution des colonies aux guerres de l'Angleterre." He examined its genesis and growth, both in Great Britain and in the colonies. The Australian and the New Zealand reactions seemed to him healthier than ours. For in our case, he said, "L'esprit de parti, poussé à un degré d'intensité inconnu en Angleterre, et la question de races, sont deux faiblesses qui nous préparent mal à lutter contre les entreprises impérialistes" (*Grande-Bretagne et Canada*, 39). Bourassa went on to state his own position, and the primacy, obvious to him, of Canada as a motherland:

Le seul terrain sur lequel il soit possible de placer la solution de nos problèmes nationaux, c'est celui du respect mutuel à nos sympathies de races et du devoir exclusif à la patrie commune. Il n'y a ici ni maîtres, ni valets, ni vainqueurs, ni vaincus: il y a deux alliés dont l'association s'est conclue sur des bases équitables et bien définies. . . .

Le sol canadien, son sang, ses richesses, son passé, son présent et son avenir—tout cela ne nous appartient que pour le transmettre intact à nos descendants. Je respecte et j'admire chez mon voisin l'amour qu'il porte à sa vieille et glorieuse patrie, et je le mépriserais si cet amour vibrait moins fort aux jours d'épreuve. J'attends en retour qu'il respecte la même fidélité du souvenir chez les enfants de la patrie française. Mais en dehors de ce domaine du cœur et de l'esprit, il n'y a qu'un moyen possible d'éviter des malentendus funestes, c'est que nous soyons et que nous restions tous deux exclusivement Canadiens sur le terrain constitutionnel et politique.

Did Bourassa seek complete autonomy for Canada? Independence seemed to him a matter of little urgency since Canada had no guarantee of peace either inside or outside her borders. Outside Canada, Bourassa feared the proximity "immédiat et exclusif de la république américaine," and he analyzed at great length the dangers it offered. This passage ended with the famous paragraph:

Ce que je voudrais, c'est qu'entre la vieille frégate anglaise qui menace de sombrer et le corsaire américain qui se prépare à recueillir ses épaves, nous manœuvrions notre barque avec prudence et fermeté afin qu'elle ne se laisse pas engloutir dans le gouffre de l'une ni entraîner dans le sillage de l'autre. Ne rompons pas la chaîne trop tôt, mais n'en rivons pas follement les anneaux.

This paragraph is the conclusion of a very close analysis of the risks incurred by a premature emancipation. As for peace within the country:

Tant qu'une entente plus franche et plus nette n'existera pas entre les deux races—et ce but désirable ne sera atteint que le jour où le peuple canadien aura forcé ses hommes d'Etat à adopter une politique canadienne, je dis que nous ne sommes pas mûrs pour l'indépendance.

One may rest assured that this passionate lover of Canadian autonomy would never wantonly stir up the two races against one another.

The following year, at the National Monument, Bourassa exam

ined "Le patriotisme Canadien-Français, ce qu'il est, ce qu'il doit être." He set forth our duty toward Great Britain (loyalty to the Crown, a matter of reason), toward English Canadians (neither fusion nor isolation; "nous devons chercher tous les terrains communs où il nous est possible de donner la main à nos concitoyens anglais sans faillir à notre dignité et sans altérer notre individualité nationale"), toward Canada (moderate federalism), and toward ourselves. He asserted in clear terms that we must be Canadians before being either Frenchmen or Englishmen.

Observe the following notation on a theme which Bourassa was to orchestrate later, but which expressed at the time both his pride and his sense of moderation:

C'est du reste, sur ce terrain de la nationalité que se manifestent les excès dangereux que j'ai signalés tantôt: l'avilissement en face des Anglais, la haine et l'injure dès qu'ils ont le dos tourné. L'instinct de race est, comme tous les instincts naturels, un puissant moyen d'action individuelle et sociale; mais, comme les autres instincts, il doit être contrôlé et tempéré par la raison. Sinon, il peut conduire à des erreurs funestes et devenir l'agent le plus efficace de notre désagrégation nationale.

The Nationalist League was founded in 1903. Henri Bourassa expounded his programme in Quebec City on December 8 of that year, and in Montreal on February 21, 1904. He began by asserting that he was not concerned with a "mouvement de race," but above all else with a protest against British imperialism. Moreover, he said he defended the same ideas in the English provinces and found followers even in Toronto.

In saying this, Bourassa fully realized that he was going against a well established French-Canadian tradition. A veteran newspaperman, J. P. Tardivel, drew this fact to Bourassa's attention in his daily, *La Vérité*. "Notre nationalisme à nous," wrote Tardivel in reply to Bourassa, "c'est le nationalisme *canadien-français*. Nous travaillons, depuis 23 ans, au développement du sentiment national *canadien-français:* ce que nous voulons voir fleurir, c'est le patriotisme *canadien-français*..." (*La Vérité*, 1 April, 1904, p. 5). Thus, he who was to be considered later the leader of French-Canadian nationalism was first accused of deviating from it. His attacker was an old crusading patriot.

Did Bourassa accept the blow? He first answered:

La Ligue Nationaliste et son organe veulent incontestablement "travailler au développement d'un sentiment canadien;" mais loin de vouloir développer ce sentiment "indépendamment de toute question d'origine, de langue, de religion," la Ligue Nationaliste proclame hautement que la dualité d'origine, de langue et de religion du peuple canadien doit être reconnue et conservée.

[*Le Nationaliste,* 3 April, 1904, p. 2]

But the Nationalist League (that is, in the present case, Bourassa) intended to overlay French-Canadian patriotism with a patriotism "plus général":

Notre nationalisme à nous est le nationalisme canadien, fondé sur la dualité des races et sur les traditions particulières que cette dualité comporte.... Les *nôtres,* pour nous comme pour M. Tardivel, sont les Canadiens français; mais les Anglo-Canadiens ne sont pas des étrangers.... La patrie, pour nous, c'est le Canada tout entier, c'est-à-dire une fédération de races distinctes et de provinces autonomes. La nation que nous voulons voir se développer, c'est la nation canadienne, composée des Canadiens français et des Canadiens anglais, c'est-à-dire de deux éléments séparés par la langue et la religion, et par les dispositions légales nécessaires à la conservation de leurs traditions respectives, mais unies dans un attachement de confraternité, dans un commun attachement à la patrie commune.

Laurier and Mr. Louis Saint-Laurent, a few words excepted, might have signed this page—and possibly Cartier. But Bourassa's political career supplied a context which one must take into account.

When Bourassa proclaims that he is first a Canadian, his Canadianism, it must be noted, does not float between heaven and earth. There were simply for him two ways of living it: one French and one English. He does not advocate a fusion; he is clearsighted enough to see that any fusion would favour the group that is stronger in number and wealth. "La patrie" is for him "le Canada tout entier"; but Canada is "une fédération de races distinctes et de provinces autonomes." He believes in the Canadian nation but sees it composed of French Canadians and

English Canadians—"c'est-à-dire de deux éléments séparés [the word is strong] par la langue et la religion, et par les dispositions légales nécessaires à la conservation de leurs traditions." (Canadian patriotism is therefore not a renunciation but an extension of the love one bears one's own. Canadian patriotism unites two entities which differ from one another, but which join again "dans un commun attachement à la patrie commune." In a word, Bourassa proclaims himself a Canadian first, but not merely a Canadian. He believes in a hyphenated patriotism, and in this kind of patriotism only. The word "Canadian" is the common denominator for people who are not in themselves common denominators. Canadian and French Canadian, Canadian and English Canadian are realities that are organically linked to each other. "Canadian" means, above all else, the acceptance of one group by the other, with the legitimate sacrifices that any marriage must entail.

The marriage adjustment is rarely accomplished with ease, and the following year was to afford proof of the matter. In 1905 the Canadian government divided the Northwest Territories into provinces (Saskatchewan and Alberta). After first attempting to deal justly with the minorities, Laurier made concessions to Sifton and to Anglo-Protestant opinion. Bourassa, both in parliament and in Quebec, upheld the Catholic and French-Canadian thesis. In sum, he told the English-Canadian members of parliament that the west promised a tremendous future; if they wished it to be Canadian they must make it attractive to French Canadians. Bourassa saw "avec douleur" the development in Quebec of "le sentiment que le Canada n'est pas le Canada de tous les Canadiens." We were being made provincials against our will.

Many of Bourassa's western adversaries, of course, opposed him in the name of "provincial autonomy"—the provinces were to have exclusive rights in matters of education. Included in their views, apparently, was the right to crush minorities. At this juncture Bourassa raised his voice and had some harsh things to say about Confederation; but he refused to attack the principle of provincial autonomy or, at the same time, to retreat to the province of Quebec. Thus, in 1912, during the new affair of the Northwest, he had this to say:

144

Français, nous avons le droit de l'être par la langue; catholiques, nous avons le droit de l'être par la foi; libre, nous avons le droit de l'être par la constitution; *Canadiens, nous le sommes avant tout;* britanniques, nous avons autant le droit de l'être que qui que ce soit. Et ces "droits," nous avons le droit d'en jouir dans toute l'étendue de la Confédération. [*Pour la justice,* speech delivered at the National Monument, 9 March, 1912, p. 33]

In the midst of war, at a time when name-calling was the fashion and the words "traitor" or "Prussian" were bandied about freely, Bourassa asserted anew that "le Canada doit transmettre aux générations à venir de son peuple les avantages inappréciables de sa double origine. . . ." For,

Rien n'est plus stérile, rien n'est plus faible et grotesque à mes yeux que d'attiser les haines de races et de baser sur les errements des individus, quelque nombreux et puissants qu'ils paraissent pour l'instant, le jugement qu'on doit porter sur toute une race. [*Le Devoir, son origine, son passé, son avenir,* speech delivered at the National Monument, 14 January, 1915]

These assertions were double-edged: first and foremost, Bourassa defended the rights of his own, and his own, as he had already made clear, were the French Canadians; but he always chose to do so in terms that were valid for all.

Bourassa was in fact always guided by the same spirit, whether he spoke in French or in English (see, for example, *French and English,* a reprint of articles, and *Ireland and Canada,* a speech given in Hamilton on St. Patrick's Day). Even when his theme led him to use harsh words against English Canadians, the tone was never one of rupture. He denounced racial prejudice wherever he found it—even within his audiences, which he often reprimanded. He attacked the British so-called spirit of fair play, and went so far as to equate English with Protestantism and French with Catholicism. His historical summaries tended to become indictments of the British, and he preached "la résistance à la domination anglo-canadienne." These more extreme views may have been due to exasperation provoked by the war and by By-Law XVII. Bourassa, however, did not let his basic conviction be shaken:

Pour nous, Messieurs, vous savez à quelle enseigne nous logeons. Canadiens, avant d'être Français ou Britanniques ... nous croyons que notre premier devoir appartient à la patrie où Dieu nous a fait naître, où six générations nous attachent au sol. [*Le Devoir et la guerre*, banquet speech, 12 January, 1916, pp. 39-40]

Certainly he railed against imperialism and against the "fureur tyrannique et tracassière" of the Ontario persecutors. But he did not forget to reaffirm that these sentiments of the moment did not make him deviate from the path he had traced. And when the drama of conscription took place, at the very hour when people from Ontario and certain westerners sought his arrest, was it not moving to hear him say, as though he were unaware of what he saw only too well, as though he were immersed in his idealism and his dream of Canadianism:

J'appartiens à l'école, moins nombreuse qu'on ne le pense, qui voit plus d'avantages que d'inconvénients dans la co-existence des deux races au Canada. Avec un nombre plus restreint encore, j'estime que le Canada tout entier bénéficiera de cette situation et recevra des deux races le maximum de leur apport au patrimoine politique, intellectuel et moral de la nation, dans l'exacte mesure où chacune d'elles restera le plus complètement elle-même.

[*La Conscription,* 1917, p. 20]

His most severe indictment of Confederation was to be formulated in 1921, in *La presse catholique et nationale.* "L'œuvre," he was to say then, "a lamentablement avorté"—has failed both from the standpoint of exterior evolution (imperialism) and interior peace. With some bitterness he outlined the circumstances surrounding this failure. One almost feels that, wounded by the experience, he is about to modify his political creed. But he takes hold of himself on the last page:

En dépit des désenchantements du passé et des sombres perspectives d'avenir, il faut penser et agir comme s'il était encore possible de faire une patrie canadienne, de créer un patriotisme national. Quelle que soit la destinée prochaine ou lointaine du Canada et de la province de Québec, tout effort persévérant pour maintenir ou faire revivre les conditions de l'accord de 1865 aura sa pleine valeur.

146

Thus Bourassa went so far as to doubt—which is, if I may say so, the method of lucid idealists. To do as if, to act as if despite the pressure of the facts the dream could still come true. It is perhaps the only way to make the dream come true.

For we must not forget that during this whole period Bourassa fought incessantly for French-Canadian causes. He did so logically; his very definition of nationalism compelled him to do so, even though, as we have seen, and especially during a war, such logic is torture. Observe the man, for instance, as he plunged into provincial politics and defended the French-Canadian homeland with all his usual ardour. To the extent that economic questions interested him (and this was not much, since he was no innovator and accepted practically all the rather undeveloped ideas of his time), to this extent only did he wish to labour for the economic progress of his own people. When he spoke of provincial autonomy he did not speak with the fire of a Mercier or of a Canon Groulx; yet he never accepted any diminution of the statehood of Quebec. He gave the best of himself, at least up to 1923, in the defence of the language; and when fatigue overwhelmed him he gave up neither his support of French schools nor his passionate love of the French language. He was possessed by a pride that took offence easily. No power, except the Church and his own convictions, ever made him bend. He claimed that people accepted him as he was—and he was a French Canadian, bound to his own. Some of his most beautiful flights of oratory express precisely this refusal to bend before a majority; he was a French-Canadian patriot because he banished from his life all cowardice. His was a noble sentiment, tainted neither with bitterness nor pettiness. But should his group be treacherously attacked, he vibrated to the depths of his being.

Bourassa belonged to his environment; he accepted and loved it, even though he judged and whipped it. The pettiness of our politicians has never been scourged so harshly as by him. Our intellectual destitution, the rancidness of our small provincial gatherings, these he soon detected, and obviously they disgusted him. He loved the affairs of French Canada as one loves one's family, though I think he found them rather narrow. He always gives one the impression of a lively fellow who would like to launch out into the world; broad syntheses were his true domain, and he was never so much at ease as in the realm of international politics. In a sense, no matter how involved he was, Bourassa the man always kept, in the face of the temporal causes he defended, the freedom of a lord. He was not their slave; he consented to defend them. Hence the offhand tone, the natural disrespect for usurped glory (even when the glory belonged to his own group), and the unexpected that keeps cropping up in his works. Yes, he had a universal mind; he was passionately interested in world affairs, though he could approach them only through London, where our colonial voice was silenced. Here again pride appears to me as the sentimental origin of his outright rejection of imperialism—and of annexation with the United States.

French-Canadian tradition was anti-imperialist, and for this reason Bourassa was to find the bulk of his followers in Quebec. On this point he got along well with French-Canadian nationalists. But the securing of Canadian independence tended to become, from the human standpoint, his primary motive, and this incited him to seek closer ties with English Canadians. He had been quick to understand that we cannot acquire independence if French Canadians and English Canadians spend all their time squabbling: emancipation implied a strong degree of Canadian unity. Here begins, perhaps, his break with French-Canadian nationalists, who are that only or principally that.

Life indeed plunges us into many contradictions. Bourassa, who wanted to unify all Canadians, had to spend a great deal of his energy on battles between Canadians. English Canadians, for example, came around to his view of imperialism only very much later; in the meantime his rather brusque frankness and his belligerent temperament offended them. His campaign for "l'égalité des races" earned him deadly enemies in all provinces. Yet, as we have seen, he clung unwaveringly to his Canadian inspiration.

It is little wonder that he had sometimes the sense of battering against a stone wall. In 1905, defending the fate of French Catholics in the west, Bourassa's magnificent analysis fell upon a hostile parliament. In the wake of several interruptions, he said suddenly: "Je sais que mes paroles seront vaines. . . . " He scented failure. He was to experience many more failures on the same subject, for although his eloquence fascinated English Canadians, it never convinced them at the time. Is it not to be expected that to a man of action who has suffered such setbacks complete provincial autonomy or separatism will appear the only alternative? When events proved to this high-strung man that French-Canadian minorities could not obtain justice anywhere—whether in Manitoba, Saskatchewan, Alberta, Ontario, or New Brunswick— would there not be a natural temptation to break with the federal regime? Bourassa, however, never seems to have seriously considered this hypothesis. No matter how strongly he asserted his French Canadianism, he had chosen to be Canadian and could not see how it could be otherwise. In accents that reveal the same indescribable pride, like a thoroughbred that rears against the bridle, he pleaded always for an autonomous country, a truly bilingual one in which religions would be truly free. Always doors were shut in his face, but always he remained stubbornly insistent on his twofold purpose. He explained his defeats and began anew. Never has there been so conscientious and so stubborn a Canadian.

Bourassa was to turn fiercely against those of his allies who, drawing their own conclusions from his repeated failures and his slight influence on English Canadians, began to argue for separatism. But before touching on that crisis I should like to examine briefly one other aspect of the question: Bourassa's religion.

Bourassa was always deeply religious—a liberal ultramontane whom Laurier called "le castor rouge." Moral issues had interested him from early youth, but as he grew older he insisted more and more on giving them first place. We have very few documents at our disposal for the analysis of such an intimate and profound sentiment. We do not know to what extent such factors as deaths in the family, personal hardship, the fatigue which stems from an active public life and marks the vanity of it all, the awareness of heavy responsibilities already assumed, as well as still more intimate factors such as the obvious tendency to scruples, which he freely acknowledged, may have awakened his religious conscience and led to great anxiety. Instead of indulging in guesswork about such matters, I prefer to state that we know very little about them. On the other hand, it is certainly possible to see in Bourassa's writings an increasing preoccupation with a moral and religious thought which is

149

becoming keener and which is nourished by a deep inner life.

Matters of language and faith are never separated in a mind such as Bourassa's. For one thing, faith is at home everywhere. Moreover, the very conditions of French life in Canada imply a relation between the two that is both unusual and vigorous. Bourassa had often faced the problem. It is at the root of his famous speech in Notre Dame Church in 1910. Let me recall the circumstances behind this discourse, which impressed the French Canadians of the time in an extraordinary manner. The occasion was a solemn one: a Eucharistic Congress had brought pilgrims to Montreal from the world over, and amongst them were important members of the Roman Catholic hierarchy. The principal speeches were to be given in Notre Dame Church. The crowd, having listened to several of the speakers, was suddenly aware that something remarkable was happening. To the amazement of the informed, the Archbishop of Westminster, Mgr Francis Bourne, was echoing a thesis on assimilation proposed by some American bishops—the thesis that the future of Catholicism lay exclusively with the English language. Bourassa improvised a fiery reply which astounded his audience, and of which eye-witnesses still speak with deep emotion. Yet his thought was remarkably moderate. Such ease of expression, without one false note and in the midst of an improvisation on such a complex theme, could only have stemmed from an already intense interior life and a sound grasp of doctrine.

Bourassa's thesis, seen through the colder medium of print, is the following:

L'Eglise catholique, précisément parce qu'elle est catholique, n'est et ne sera jamais l'Eglise d'une époque, d'un pays, d'une nation.... Mais si l'Eglise ne peut être la chose d'une race ou d'une nation, elle les reconnaît toutes, les respecte et les protège également—les victorieuses et les vaincues, les fortes et les faibles, les riches et les pauvres.

The Church, he goes on, consents to adjust herself to the various groups; but

[Elle] ne peut être ni française ni anglaise. Elle ne peut non plus asservir une race à l'autre.

Lier la cause de l'Eglise à celle de la race et de la langue française au Canada serait une erreur. Faire de l'Eglise un instrument d'assimilation anglo-saxonne serait également absurde et odieux.

[*Le Devoir*, 20 July, 1910]

However, in the case of the French Canadians, it so happens that the language is the guardian of the faith: Bourassa established this in 1918 in a brochure entitled *La langue gardienne de la foi*, the arguments of which have become familiar to all French Canadians. He unfolded these arguments through a careful choice of words and with great caution; the limits of the thesis are just as carefully delineated as the thesis itself. Nevertheless, for him the French language, "la vraie langue française," is a "véhicule de la foi." He eulogizes it in pages that reveal his love of clearness, of order, and of rational values. Undoubtedly, next to "la vraie langue française" is another language which for two centuries has been "la langue du mal et de l'Esprit du mal, la langue de l'enfer et de Satan. *Corruptio optimi pessima*." But French Canadians have escaped this contamination. Moreover, "notre tâche à nous, Canadiens français, c'est de prolonger en Amérique l'effort de la France chrétienne; c'est de défendre contre tout venant, le fallut-il contre la France elle-même, notre patrimoine religieux et national." This inheritance remains a radiant source of inspiration for the whole of Catholic America. We alone can fulfil this task in America. We shall fulfil it if we keep our language pure, and, above all, our faith alive. Taken as a whole, this text was in line with the speech in Notre Dame; but it pushed the conclusions of the latter somewhat further, tending to grant more weight to the language itself, and later, in 1935, Bourassa was to feel the need to disavow certain pages despite the fact that the bulk of it was well thought out and marked with charity for the nationalities he happened to refer to.

During the years immediately following the war, it seems to me, though I may be wrong, that Bourassa's thought is inspired more directly and more literally by the dicta of the Popes. Was it that the world conflict made him disgusted with temporal things, so that he found in the appeals of Benedict XV for peace a particularly warm inspiration? Was he disturbed by his differences with a part of the hierarchy on wartime problems (that is to say, on a subject where Catholics are free) and therefore felt the need to seek the immediate support of the leader of Catholicism? It can only be a question of emphasis with this long-standing ultramontane, but I think one can detect here a more eager meditation of the pontifical writings.

Bourassa went on studying, became more concerned than ever about doctrine, used his knowledge of history to furnish himself with precedents and warnings. At the same time he became more isolated, more inclined to follow his own path.

Then occurred an event which Bourassa subsequently and on several occasions described and which seemed to polarize all his fears: a private audience with Pius XI during his trip to Rome in 1926. It will not do either to underrate or overrate the importance of this event. The founder of *Le Devoir*, the creator of a new nationalism, listened for an hour to "une conférence sur ce qu'il y a de légitime et d'illégitime [dans] le nationalisme contemporain." It was certainly a shock; but Bourassa was ready to listen to what the head of Christianity had to tell him. This will be seen in a moment in a text of 1920. The point is that after this long and potent interview Bourassa was to consider himself entrusted with a very definite mission.

The first sign of a break with his disciples I find in an article written by Bourassa in 1920—six years, in other words, before his audience with Pius XI:

... On ne saurait trop répéter que la lutte pour la langue et la culture française, légitimes en soi, n'est qu'*accessoire* et subordonnée à la lutte pour la foi et le droit paternel. On ne saurait trop redire que la langue française et les traditions canadiennes-françaises doivent être conservées surtout parce qu'elles constituent de précieux éléments de l'ordre social catholique. Certains défenseurs très ardents de la langue semblent l'oublier; ou du moins leurs activités un peu étroites tendent à obscurcir ces notions dans l'esprit du peuple.

[*Le Devoir*, 9 November, 1920]

This passage seems to me significant. By and large it does not contradict any of Bourassa's former statements (except for the use of the word "accessory," which I have italicized), but it does show how the emphasis is shifting. The struggles for the French language and culture are "légitimes en soi"—and we shall do well to remember these words, for they are not written absentmindedly:

Bourassa believes in the legitimacy of the struggles he has fought. Only, as he grows older, he gives them less importance, considering their objective subordinate to the objective of the struggle for the faith. He goes so far as to declare the former objective "accessoire," thus depriving it of any intrinsic value; language and traditions are to be preserved *especially* ("surtout") because they help support "l'ordre social catholique." Beneath these words, I may say, is to be found a religious view which I once tagged with the general term of Jansenism—a view which consists in debasing the intrinsic value of the creature and granting him only such value as is a direct function of the Creator. Here, Bourassa parts company not only with French-Canadian nationalists but with all Christians who acknowledge some splendour in the creature itself, and who, without denying the reference to higher authority, are unwilling to reduce the creature to a mere cipher. These are, of course, but tendencies. Finally, there is disdain in the allusion to the "activités un peu étroites," an attitude which reflects the perspective of a man who is busy with problems that are broad in scope and who finds that the affairs of French Canada are not the end of the world.

Another article, "La presse catholique et nationale," published in *Le Devoir* in 1921, contains an equally significant formulation of his views. Bourassa speaks of the Church as an international power. He goes on to quote Charles Maurras, but he introduces the quotation with this categorical judgement: "Un incroyant, imbu de nationalisme amoral et outrancier. . . . "

This brings us, indeed, to the problem of the influence exerted by Maurras, the contemporary theorist of French monarchy and of "nationalisme intégral" whom Mussolini, Salazar, and Pétain praised rather highly, upon French-Canadian nationalism in general, and in particular upon the *Action française* of Montreal, directed by Canon Groulx. I believe the influence to be less than has been thought by others, even by Bourassa himself. True, nationalist intellectuals were experiencing at this time a craze for Maurras. They read the *Action française* (from Paris) with fervour because they found in it, expressed in magnificent words, reasons to believe in French civilization, and, for some, the spell was magic. It is remarkable that Bourassa discerned from the outset what was anti-Christian and excessive in Maurras. He reacted with a kind of sacred fury against what appeared to him as a deviation from the religious way, against a positivist form of rightist Catholicism such as was later condemned by Pius XI.

One can well imagine what this feeling was to become when Bourassa thought he discerned in the Montreal *Action française* a plea for separatism. (The 1922 inquiry on "Notre avenir politique" is worth rereading; it is not really a plea for secession, but it undoubtedly reflects separatist ferment.) Here were former disciples not only seeking their emancipation—and despite his noble character it is likely that he suffered from this—but seeking also a solution which, as far back as 1904, he had rejected in opposing Tardivel. A good deal of time, however, had elapsed since then. An older, more taut Bourassa, one who is a little testy in his faith, faces younger men whose source of inspiration he suspects. The dim intuitions of Tardivel have now become a system of thought that is vaguely heretical in his eyes. There is nothing surprising in Bourassa's reaction. The Canadian nationalism to which he had dedicated himself at the outset, his fear of revolutions (in other words, the fear of becoming a second Papineau), and the manner in which he understands the demands of Christianity—all these coalesce within him to reject this new orientation.

Bourassa had indeed noted "la banqueroute de la confédération," but he never wanted to give up. He still clung through sheer will, even during the hours of black disenchantment, to the idea of a Canadian homeland. He did not take separatism seriously. He took too seriously the Maurassian spirit of our *Action française*. And because he took it seriously, on 18 April, 1923, in the second of his discourses on "Le Pape, médecin social," he attacked. He denounced the "nationalisme immodéré" of which he had found traces up till then; and he continued in words which *Le Devoir* summarized as follows:

> Pas d'antagonisme envers les autres groupes canadiens, pas de politique d'isolement pour le Québec, non, non. Trente ans d'études convainquent l'orateur qu'il n'y a rien de plus dangereux, de plus irréalisable que le séparatisme. Ce serait déchaîner la guerre civile, semer les divisions dans nos rangs, nuire aux autres groupes français d'Amérique, nous heurter à des forces qui nous écraseraient.

154

Nous avons triomphé de l'assimilation en gardant à la lutte son carac-
tère catholique, en maintenant le lien constant entre le droit de parler
sa langue et de conserver sa foi. Pas de haine pour les autres catholiques, pas d'isolement de la tour ivoire, pas d'orgueil de race supérieure,
pas de pharisaïsme à la façon d'Israël qui a perdu ses droits pour avoir
voulu accaparer Dieu.

But the attitude of French-Canadian nationalism is also quite
understandable. The new separatist thrust (we have already seen
that the expression is too strong) came in the wake of Bourassa's
action, after his battles in favour of minorities—none of which,
it must be remembered, had been fully victorious, or at least had
not been to that moment, for the repeal of By-Law XVII was to
come later. The disciples, consciously or not, took note of these
failures, and their drift towards separatism took root in despair.
They had in large measure lost faith in the capacity of Confederation to render justice, in its ability to function smoothly, and finally in the very idea of a Canadianism now considered exclusively
English-Canadian. They no longer saw how French Canada could
live freely in the midst of Canada; and they were at the same time
convinced that Canada, a geographical absurdity, and the British
Empire, alike divided by internal forces of dissension, could not
long survive post-war readjustments. But Bourassa himself always
refused to despair. Though he recorded the bankruptcy of Confederation, he did not fully believe that it had come to this. He
considered the proposed solution of separatism, moreover, unfortunate and out of touch with reality.

Bourassa expressed his views again in a speech of November 23,
1923, that was broader and more temperate. He noted once again
that few Canadians were really Canadians, and underscored the
dangers of a narrow and obstinate provincialism. His denunciation of separatism as "ni réalisable, ni souhaitable" is lively, precise,
and sound, but in no way high-handed. He reaffirmed that we
are first of all Canadians, and he defined once more the elements
of his nationalism: one is a matter of exterior liberty—that is,
the rejection of British imperialism; the other is interior and
involves a conception of a "juste équilibre entre les deux races."
And both questions remain linked together: imperialism can be
vanquished only through "l'association des deux races-mères."

His nationalism, then, remained active, vigilant, and vigorous, even in matters French-Canadian; but he watched its expression more carefully, and one feels that he was less involved in the venture. The tone is somewhat cooler.

We seem to be left with a paradox. Here is a man who unceasingly held for "les siens" an obvious preferential love, yet who was at the same time a founder of Canadian nationalism and who took the French-Canadian nationalist movement as one of his favourite targets. Indeed, his opposition to the provincial movement in the end took on the character of an open and bitter fight. But it might become tedious to carry the analysis further. I think we now hold, at least partially, an explanation of it all. The paradox is only apparent. Bourassa's contradictions come principally from the type of double allegiance that he had accepted from the outset—that is, from the fact that he refused to be only a Canadian, or only a French Canadian. He had decided from the beginning to be both intensely. And so quite often he seems to contradict himself—not in spite of reason, but to a large extent because he is logical.

To conclude: how does Bourassa appear to us from the vantage point of the present? Can his example serve again in a historical context that has been profoundly modified? The importance of New Canadians has increased remarkably. To the struggle for political independence from Great Britain has succeeded fear of the excessive influence (which Bourassa, however, had foreseen) of the United States. Some of the past struggles have lost their meaning: there now remains the common desire to live as Canadians. In this respect Bourassa remains a model.

What was he? First, a French Canadian. He was French to the core: nervous, a reasoner, impressionable, witty in the French manner, ironic, harsh, or violent in the French manner. Even after he had become, through admiration for the institution and application, a parliamentarian in the English manner, he had flashes of wit and humour, spurts of eloquence that broke the traditional framework and revealed the predominating strength, the will, the personal attractiveness, sometimes even the insolence, of this kind of French aristocrat. He was first a French Canadian because he had absorbed all the riches of the soil, had mingled with the

156

humble folk and acquired something of their language. Inspired
by what he called the genius of his race, he was never more
eloquent than when he exalted the language, the culture, and the
rights of his own people—never, except when he was fighting for
the liberty of his country.

Bourassa harboured a strong desire for personal independence.
He accepted but one yoke, that of the Church. Sometimes he
throbbed with impatience when he faced a cleric or a bishop who
had wandered beyond his own domain; but more often, and always
in the presence of the head of Catholicism, he submitted. And he
submitted with a literalism that surprises in a mind such as his.
Might this not be the intellectual revelation of an inner unrest
which was constantly combatted and repressed? When he submits,
he is as a little child; he accepts all—and even a little more. The
same form of submission, moreover, he preaches to his contemporaries. He remonstrates with them. Yet, though he puts his whole
heart into this and although his knowledge is great, there remains
in him an indefinable tenseness and secretiveness (in the manner
of Louis Veuillot) which prevents him from communicating the
full measure of his spiritual resources. Temporal servitude, on the
other hand, he rejected in all its forms: honours, parties, empire,
or whatever. First and above all else, he refused to be a colonial,
refused to let his country accept the destiny of colony, whether of
Great Britain or the United States. From a human standpoint,
this is his greatest battle and the work of his choice.

There can be little doubt that the British Empire itself made
of him a Canadian in the broad sense of the word. He had been
largely indebted to Laurier, I believe, for the ideal of "l'unité
nationale." Yet I doubt whether this youthful idealism alone
would have stood up under the setbacks English Canadians inflicted upon the campaigns he undertook through love of justice
and of his own people. But he was involved in a struggle which
absorbed him still more—one at the end of which he saw the
emancipation of his country, its final liberation from an unacceptable slavery. He had come to the conclusion that this would
be possible only if French Canadians and English Canadians
united. Having been convinced from his youth that separatism
was a dream that had come too late or too early, and that it was
therefore a dangerous chimera closely related to that "nationa-

lisme sauvage" which his Catholicism made him reject, he took the view that the whole of Canada would be liberated on the condition that Canadians stopped fighting one another.

At the same time, he did not reject one form of slavery to accept another: at war with the tyranny of the empire, he was not going to accept within his own race the tyranny of the majority. For him, moreover, as we have already seen, the word "Canadian" represented a friendly meeting-ground, not a ground on which there would be the type of fusion that is death to minorities. With his taste for paradox and his congenital disdain for all low forms of flattery, he willingly preached, and preached increasingly, Canadianism to French Canadians and the rights of French Canadians to English Canadians. French Canadian by instinct, moved at times by necessity and at other times by a dynamic faith in the Canada of tomorrow, he willingly ratified the marriage of reason between the two national collectivities which seemed to him to be imposed by the facts.

But nothing was to satisfy fully such an exacting mind, nothing but the absolute. Bourassa's religious thought deepened progressively. Little by little everything else, in spite of some glowing embers, appeared to him of small worth. Some thought the man was contradicting himself, but that was an oversimplification. He evolved indeed, but never to the point of compromising his basic ideas.

"The point about Bourassa," a professor at the University of Toronto has just written to one of my friends, "is that he does not belong to French Canada alone." This is true. Through his struggles, Bourassa belongs to the whole of Canada. He is a magnificent example of a Canadian: he is the man who rejects all forms of slavery, but who accepts all forms of loyalty. His dedication to Canada was not prefaced by his surrender as a French Canadian. He is a man who sits at the common table but who does not choose to let himself be forgotten. He wants to be welcomed, not exploited, and he wants to be accepted as he is, in the same way that he himself loyally accepts his partner. Such is, I believe, the nationalism of Bourassa which divided his contemporaries but which will contribute to uniting Canadians of today.